SEMEIA 42

Reasoning with the Foxes
Female Wit in a World of Male Power

> There is Reason, asserting itself as above the world, and there is Reason as one of many factors within the world. The Greeks have bequeathed to us two figures, whose real or mythical lives conform to these two notions—Plato and Ulysses. The one shares Reason with the Gods, the other shares it with the foxes.
>
> —Alfred North Whitehead,
> *The Function of Reason*

Editors of This Issue:
J. Cheryl Exum and Johanna W. H. Bos

©1988
by the Society of Biblical Literature

SEMEIA 42

Copyright © 1988 by the Society of Biblical Literature

All rights reserved. No part of this work may be reproduced or transmitted in any form or by any means, electronic or mechanical, including photocopying and recording, or by means of any information storage or retrieval system, except as may be expressly permitted by the 1976 Copyright Act or in writing from the publisher. Requests for permission should be addressed in writing to the Rights and Permissions Office, Society of Biblical Literature, 825 Houston Mill Road, Atlanta, GA 30329, USA.

ISSN 0095-571X
ISBN 1-58983-154-3

Printed in the United States of America
on acid-free paper

CONTENTS

Contributors to This Issue v

Preface vii

ARTICLES

Israelite Tricksters,
Their Analogues and Cross-cultural Study
  Naomi Steinberg 1

Wise and Strange: An Interpretation of the Female Imagery
in Proverbs in Light of Trickster Mythology
  Claudia V. Camp 14

Out of the Shadows:
Genesis 38; Judges 4:17-22; Ruth 3
  Johanna W. H. Bos 37

"For I Have the Way of Women":
Deception, Gender, and Ideology in Biblical Narrative
  Esther Fuchs 68

The Deceptive Goddess in Ancient Near Eastern Myth:
Inanna and Inaraš
  Carole Fontaine 84

RESPONSES

Interrogating Biblical Deception and Trickster Theories:
Narratives of Patriarchy or Possibility?
  Kathleen M. Ashley 103

Deception and Women: A Response
  Edwin M. Good 117

Tricky Thematics
  Mieke Bal 133

trickster tumbles
  Carole Fontaine 156

CONTRIBUTORS TO THIS ISSUE

Kathleen M. Ashley
Department of English
University of Southern Maine
Gorham, ME 04038

Mieke Bal
Department of Foreign Languages, Literatures and Linguistics
University of Rochester
Rochester, NY 14627

Johanna W. H. Bos
Louisville Presbyterian Theological Seminary
1044 Alta Vista Road
Louisville, KY 40205

Claudia V. Camp
Department of Religion-Studies
Texas Christian University
Fort Worth, TX 76129

J. Cheryl Exum
Department of Theology
Boston College
Chestnut Hill, MA 02167

Carole Fontaine
Andover Newton Theological School
Newton Centre, MA 02159

Esther Fuchs
Department of Oriental Studies
The University of Arizona
Tucson, AZ 85721

Edwin M. Good
Department of Religious Studies
Stanford University
Stanford, CA 94305

Naomi Steinberg
Department of Religious Studies
DePaul University
Chicago, IL 60614

PREFACE

No, we are not suggesting a Whiteheadian approach to biblical literature. Nor is our title and our selection of these lines from Whitehead as our epigraph—a metaphor which allows him to distinguish theoretical from practical reasoning—intended to stereotype biblical women as devious or cunning, or concerned only with immediate results. Rather, Whitehead's association of "reasoning with the foxes" with seeking an immediate method of action as opposed to seeking a complete understanding seemed to us a fanciful point of departure for a volume of essays exploring a particular and prevalent characterization of the female in biblical and ancient Near Eastern texts. Because of their subordinate status, women in this body of literature frequently rely on indirect means to accomplish their goals; deception and trickery often feature significantly in their stories. Men use these indirect means too, of course (see, for example, David Marcus, "David the Deceiver and David the Dupe," *Prooftexts* 6 [1986], 163-71), and some of the analyses here specifically raise the question of the role gender plays in such characterization. Consideration of cross-cultural studies of the Trickster figure also prove useful in illuminating the biblical and ancient Near Eastern characterizations, though the limitations of cross-cultural comparison must be acknowledged.

A major concern of this volume has been to foster cross-disciplinary stimulation and interdisciplinary dialogue. All the essays in this volume make use of various literary, folkloristic, sociological or anthropological approaches. The articles and one of the responses are written by biblical scholars; two responses are by scholars outside the field of biblical studies. They suggest that much can be learned by paying attention to the assessment of similar issues in other fields.

Finally, these essays represent feminist criticism in various exploratory stages. They illustrate emerging methodologies and concerns which, we believe, move feminist discussion in biblical criticism significantly forward. As these essays suggest, the powerful intellectual challenge posed by feminism to the established critical principles of academic discourse remains to be felt in its full force.

J. Cheryl Exum

ISRAELITE TRICKSTERS, THEIR ANALOGUES AND CROSS-CULTURAL STUDY

Naomi Steinberg
DePaul University

ABSTRACT

Trickster tales are understood by anthropologists, folklorists, and historians of religions to be the expression of social concerns in narrative form. This article examines how the figure of the trickster functions in West African and Afro-American folklore and considers the importance of the comical in the development of his character. The role of the trickster in the Hebrew Bible is discussed in light of this cross-cultural evidence, with special interest in women as tricksters in ancient Israel. Analysis of the biblical material suggests that the role of trickster is available to both men and women and that trickery is used in situations where other forms of power are lacking. Stories of tricksters in the Bible appear to be explorations of the instability of the power brokers in society. The different functions of the trickster in different contexts suggest that cross-cultural analysis of the figure be avoided until the meaning of the trickster in each society where it appears is better understood.

1.1   On Trickster proceeded. As he walked along, he came to a lovely piece of land. There he sat down and soon fell asleep. After a while he woke up and found himself lying on his back, without a blanket. He looked up above him and saw to his astonishment something floating there. "Aha, aha! The chiefs have unfurled their banner! The people must be having a great feast for this is always the case when the chief's banner is unfurled." With this he sat up and then first realized that his blanket was gone. It was his blanket he saw floating above. His penis had become stiff and the blanket had been forced up. "That's always happening to me," he said. "My younger brother, you will lose the blanket, so bring it back." Thus he spoke to his penis. Then he took hold of it and, as he handled it, it got softer and the blanket finally fell down. Then he coiled up his penis and put it in a box. And only when he came to the end of his penis did he find his blanket. The box with the penis he carried on his back (Radin: 18-19).

1.2   This episode in the cycle of the trickster of whom the Winnebago Indians tell is exemplary of the tales told of this comical figure by traditional societies. The trickster is lusty and loud, a destroyer and a creator, both stupid and clever, but always comical. The trickster appears sometimes as demigod, sometimes as animal, e.g., coyote or rabbit, and sometimes as human. Yet, to speak of the trickster is to speak of a creation of folklorists, anthropologists, and historians of religions, for, in fact, the so-called trickster tales analyzed by scholars typically contain no explicit reference to such a figure.

1.3   Historically, the label "trickster" first entered scholarly discussion when Daniel Brinton applied it to the chief character in North American Indian stories; it appears to have become part of academic vocabulary by the end of the nineteenth century (Pelton: 6). More recently, the trickster is understood to be a character type based on criteria developed within the scholarly community. Not surprisingly then, trickster is a term applied to figures which come in widely diverse guises and is a scholarly generalization based on data observed cross-culturally.

1.4   In an attempt to move our discussion forward, it will be helpful to have some working definition of this elusive character as he is found among traditional societies. Most would concur that trickster refers to a shaper of culture, a transformer of boundaries, a link between the sacred and the profane.

> Tricksters are breakers of rules, but, though they are often tragic in their own specific way, their breaking of rules is always comical. This funny irregularity is the central quality of the trickster; and what makes the anomie comical is the trickster's lowliness. When he is an animal, the trickster is a crafty, rather than a powerful, beast (in this respect, it should be noted that the trickster is a wolf only where the animal kingdom is dominated by the kingly lion); when a human being, he never ranks high, and his power lies in his witty brain or in some strange gift of nature. So a working definition of the trickster could be: "a breaker of rules who is funny because he is lowly" (Grottanelli: 120).

1.51   The analogue of the trickster has been applied from American Indian tales to figures from West African narratives and then to ancient, medieval, and modern stories. Analyses of these tricksters are ultimately focused on understanding the "meaning" of this creature. Theories to explain the social role of trickster narratives vary, ranging from pure entertainment to a psychological steam-valve for critiquing social values to a means of testing and expanding social boundaries. What most of these explanations share is a concern with one who is marginal, either for a period of time or as a temporary state (Babcock-Abrahams: 148-58).

1.52 For example, a recent study of the trickster tales among the Ashante, Fon, Yoruba and Don of West Africa provides extensive analysis of the function of the theriomorphic creatures around whom these cycles revolve. According to historian of religions Robert Pelton, the West Africans who tell trickster stories understand them ultimately as stories about transcending the boundaries of life. The trickster figure represents "the transforming power of the human imagination" (Pelton: 256). In particular, the trickster is a transformer of boundaries in the name of hope, of life in process, of life that encompasses suffering and even death.

> His mockery includes himself, for he literally makes fun of the hidden underside of life, even his own. As the trickster exposes that dirty bottom, he invites man to contemplate what he shall become and to hope for what he already is—a world large in its intricacy, spiritual in its crude bodiliness, multiple in its ironic wholeness, and finally transcendent in the very absurdity of its pretensions (Pelton: 264-65).

1.61 The same analytic category "trickster" appears in discussions about Southern slave society in this country. For Afro-Americans, the notion of the trickster provided a psychological defense mechanism against the evils of the social system of slavery. In speaking of how slaves dealt with the oppression inherent in the class system in the Old South, Genovese writes:

> The holidays, like the Saturday night parties, provided the occasion for the unleashing of the satirical black story telling and singing. In the South as in the Caribbean, Brazil, and elsewhere in the Americas, slaves spun out folktales of weak creatures who outwitted oppressors and bullies by guile and trickery. In the Brer Rabbit stories, as in the Jamaican Anansi stories, the trickster, so reminiscent of African folklore, appeared everywhere. The devices for lampooning the whites took extraordinarily clever forms. Here, a body servant who had accompanied his master to France vilified the French as barbarous and ridiculous people; there, the slaves poured out scorn on the Irish in jokes that sent masters into fits of appreciative laughter. However the prejudices of the masters conspired to make these jokes acceptable, the slaves surely knew that Frenchmen and Irish-

men are white and that blacks were not supposed to ridicule any whites. The forms appear to have had African origins, but they also no doubt arose from other sources (582-83).

1.62 In the context of slavery, the figure of the trickster reveals a mechanism of praise for those who are able to turn a system of oppression on its head through ridicule of those in control. It is an expression of the values of the oppressed—both women and men—which seems to have been employed effectively. These tales of the trickster essentially represent a subversion tradition. Looked at from another perspective, structural analyses of Afro-American trickster tales suggest that inequality is central to the meaning of these stories (Edwards, 1984: 92).

1.7 From what we have seen thus far it would seem that the label "trickster" applies to a character with a complex of roles. In different contexts it would seem to have different meanings and to serve different functions. Thus, while some points of consensus have been reached on the role of the West African and Afro-American trickster, what ultimately results in scholarly literature is a shift from what is common between these peoples to what is unique about the trickster in each culture (Edwards, 1984:84). Little attention is paid to possible ways in which these figures can be related to each other. Indeed, it is worth asking whether anything connects these characters to each other, aside from the unpredictableness of their personalities. Another question that could be raised, depending on the academic discipline of the one doing the research, is whether the focus of study should be a specific character type, trickster, or a specific literary genre, trickster tale? Possibly scholarship needs to develop a taxonomy of the trickster which would allow for both the similarities and differences between these animal and human figures. It may be time to recognize that the preference shown by different cultures for different trickster types makes any universal statements about the function, and even the definition of this character impossible (Beidelman: 38; Edwards, 1984:91).

2.1 Whatever attention biblical scholars have paid to the trickster in the literature of ancient Israel has typically focused on the use of deception by women. That some recurrent role pattern exists and that it might offer clues to interpreting narrative has rarely been considered. Thus, I wish to focus on this possibility in this essay and to consider the biblical evidence in light of data on African and Afro-American tricksters. In particular, I am interested in investigating what relevance the role of the trickster has for the biblical narratives in general and for our reading of texts on women in particular. Presumably before the biblical literature was considered to be authoritative Scripture, at a time before it was contextualized as religious tradition, it, like other folklore, explicitly was recognized to refer to the sexual and the comical. With the passage of time and growing religious authority, this very human element in the literature of ancient Israel appears to have been lost or expunged, at least according to modern sensitivities.

2.2 It is important to recognize how contemporary social consciousness has influenced scholarship on the mechanism of trickery in the stories of the Bible. At the risk of oversimplification, one may argue that the changing political and social situation of men and women in the twentieth century has been mirrored in an attitude of either accommodation or resistance by biblical scholars to androcentric perspectives on the social structure of ancient Israel. Studies written prior to the 1960s were shaped by notions of patriarchy; studies written since the 1960s are marked by a decisive shift in paradigm as modern interpreters attempt to correct earlier presuppositions on the primacy of men and to affirm the place of women in the Hebrew Bible. The following two assessments of the significance of the act of deception, or the role of the trickster in the biblical world, reflect the differences in ideological orientation mentioned above:

> The man is the centre of the family, the woman his helpmeet; her desire is toward the husband, "but he rules over her." It is expressed by her being called by his name (Is. 4,1; Tob. 2,8). The will of the husband is the will of the house; the woman must often act by underhand means and use cunning in order to have her way. A typical example of this kind of woman's cunning is when Rebekah makes the blind father give Jacob his blessing. No less typical is the example of the clever Abigail, who, behind the back of her husband, tries to atone for his foolishness in relation to the strong captain of the freebooters (I Sam 25) (Pedersen: 69).

> If Rebekah's deception of her husband is an example of "women's cunning," then some of the men whose cunning is described in the Old Testament suffered from a sexual identity crisis! The list of such "feminine" males would include Abraham . . . Jacob . . . Saul . . . David. . . . This list is incomplete, but it should be enough evidence to refute the contention that cunning was a female trait in ancient Israel (Otwell: 109).

Is the enactment of the role of trickster idiosyncratic behavior peculiar to the personalities of women, as Pedersen would have it, or is it behavior appropriate to both sexes for purposes of achieving individual goals? How can one discover something meaningful about the role of the trickster in the Hebrew Bible without having the assessment depend on the presence or absence of sensitivities to the women's movement? Or, is trickery indeed a woman's issue?

3.1 Evidence from the social sciences suggests that individuals resort to the use of trickery under certain social conditions. In particular, when individuals lack authority—whether it be political, economic, religious, or domestic authority—they resort to strategies which allow them to achieve their goals and gain compliance with their wishes. I understand trickery to be a kind of power available to persons in a subordinate position vis-à-vis another individual. The classic statement of the distinction between authority and power was developed by Weber. In the words of M. G. Smith,

> Authority is, in the abstract, the right to make a particular decision and to command obedience. . . . Power . . . is the ability to act effectively on persons or things, to make or secure favorable decisions which are not of right allocated to the individuals or their roles. (18-19).

3.2 Thus, while some individuals may have a culturally legitimated right to gain compliance from others within the hierarchy governed by the roles of the society, this situation does not imply that those denied access to that authority are without recourse in attempting to gain compliance with their own interests. This exercise of power is limited only by social norms detailing "the conditions of illegality of its operation" (Smith: 20). With regard to the role of trickster, or the use of deception or subterfuge to shape events, repeated occurrences of the same behavior pattern suggest that a role significant for the perpetuation of Israelite social structure is being enacted. I am interested, therefore, in appreciating the importance of trickery as a method of achieving personal goals for any individuals in the situation of "underdog" in a social relationship.

4.1 It is impossible to give a comprehensive list of the enactment of the role of trickster in the Hebrew Bible. Some of the examples which come to mind immediately include the arguments used by the Israelite midwives to explain their inability to comply with Pharaoh's death command for Israelite male infants (Exod 1:15-19), Abraham's statement to Pharaoh and Abimelech that his wife is his sister as a tactic to save his life in a foreign land (Gen 12:10-13:1; 20:1-18), Jael's hospitality toward Sisera to gain his trust so that she can kill him while he sleeps (Judg 4:17-22; 5:24-27), the mandate that the men of the Canaanite city of Hamor be circumcised in order that some of Jacob's sons may take revenge on them at a time of physical weakness (Gen 34), Rachel's words to her father Laban to keep him from discovering that she is the one who has taken the family gods (Gen 31:33-35), and Delilah's attempts to subdue Samson as he works to keep her in ignorance about his strength (Judg 16). In each of these examples, trickery is used by a person in a position of social disadvantage in order to influence the course of events. As an additional point, one might note that the tricksters listed include both men and women. Further, each of the stories is not without a comical side to it.

4.2 We now move to consider two of these examples. The first one will be the brief conversation between Rachel and Laban as Jacob separates from his father-in-law (Gen 31:33-35). After having acquired wives, children, and property (Gen 29:1-31:16), Jacob decides it is time to declare his independence and to return to the land of Canaan. He flees from Laban without formally announcing his departure to his father-in-law, but not before Rachel has secretly stolen the teraphim belonging to the family. Whether the latter were objects of religious significance (Greenberg) or important for questions of inheritance (Draffkorn) cannot detain us here. What is interesting is the way that Rachel is so easily able to elude Laban's search for the teraphim by claiming, "the way of women is upon me" (31:35). Certainly this must be a prevarication guaranteed to get Rachel what she wants: the household gods! To those who would ask, how can we know whether she was telling the truth or not, the point is precisely that we can't. Rachel knew how to keep Laban away from her with an excuse that no one would seek to verify. Though our present state of knowledge makes it impossible to determine what the ancient Israelite knew about conception or pregnancy, the fact is that later on in the course of the journey back to Canaan, Rachel gives birth to Benjamin (35:16-18). The text does not indicate how much longer after they originally set out this event occurred; but it is possible that the notice of Benjamin's birth is the narrator's means for informing the reader that Rachel was lying all along. To be sure, this is only conjectural, but it is definitely worth considering. Her assertion can neither be proved nor denied. I would suggest, then, that we are expected to recognize the value of having a quick wit, i.e., using deceptions when necessary to influence the course of events, to keep out of trouble with one in authority. Rachel thought quickly and clearly and came up with the "right" answer for avoiding compliance with the one in a position of authority. She is the trickster who dupes the one in power! She is a trickster by means of role reversal (see below §5.4).

4.31   That we cannot determine the veracity of Rachel's statement is in every way similar to the situation with Abraham in Gen 20:12 when he claims that Sarah is his sister. The details of the so-called wife-sister story in Gen 20:1-18 are too familiar to rehearse. They concern the attempt by the patriarch Abraham to pass his wife Sarah off as his sister while in the land of Abimelech king of Gerar. I understand Abraham to be moved to do so through an interest in ridding himself of his barren wife. Without a child to validate her position in the household, Sarah is expendable to Abraham; he will find an answer to the problem of an heir without her. Under these circumstances, the woman appears to be totally vulnerable to her husband's words and actions. It is God's intervention that brings Abraham's scheme to an end and restores the conjugal unit to its original state.

4.32   What interests me most in this example is that while the patriarch tricks the foreign ruler into believing that Sarah is his sister and not his wife, he is never punished by either God or Abimelech for his words, and in fact money is given to Abraham as vindication for Sarah. At the end of the story not only are husband and wife back together, they have Abimelech's permission to move freely about his land, and are financially better off than before their adventure began. Abraham, an individual subject to the authority of the foreign ruler, resorts to trickery, displaying some quick thinking when Abimelech charges him with lying about his relationship to Sarah and thereby potentially bringing harm to Abimelech's kingdom. Abraham comes up with a response that satisfies Abimelech, which gets him off the hook, and which cannot be verified. From this example, we see another case of role reversal by means of trickery: Abimelech plays the dupe while the trickster Abraham acts as power broker.

4.4   The examples of the use of deceit in the Hebrew Bible primarily concern the use of trickery by women in their relationships with men. But I think it would be incorrect to think that women are the only ones forced to obtain power this way. The male-centeredness of much of the Bible results in a view of women as being at a social disadvantage. Given this male perspective, it is not surprising that fewer examples occur of men working to gain compliance with their wishes through trickery. The examples are there, however, and need to be recognized so that women are not stereotyped as the underhanded sex. That the trickster appears often and with impunity suggests that this role was a form of power available to those who lacked other means to achieve their goals. Especially interesting is that these tricksters are not portrayed as disruptive to social stability. Indeed, the enactment of the role of trickster results in an underdog character successfully competing against someone higher than himself/herself without the so-called superior figure even realizing that deception has occurred. Harmonious social relations are the typical result of this subterfuge.

5.1 The similarities between the trickster figures in the slave tales, in the West African stories, and in the Hebrew Bible are noticeable, and yet there are differences between the three. The most obvious of these differences is that the biblical trickster is neither demigod nor animal but rather human, either man or woman. As mentioned above, the Afro-American stories appear to provide a psychological steam valve for the oppressed to deal with their oppression while the trickster figures from West Africa embody the possibilities of transforming human boundaries and of bringing daily experiences in line with what is cosmic.

> The trickster, therefore, in juggling with his own body, in his manipulation of its parts, his toying with its wastes, his fascination with his orifices and their products, his confidence in its potencies, is the image of man in his openness to every other world and his readiness to meet and exchange with each, to be modified by each in turn (Pelton: 262).

5.21 Thus, the West African trickster offers perspective on how the individual fits into the macrocosmic picture. In contrast, it would seem that the trickster stories of the Hebrew Bible are more concerned with the microcosm of daily Israelite life. What is especially striking in the latter case is that the stories about these figures, these individuals who engage in role reversal such that the weak become the strong and the strong become the weak, were presumably told by those who held the power in the society, i.e., the men. Therefore, it is worth considering these narratives as speculation on power by the power brokers of the society. This situation distinguishes the trickster stories of ancient Israel from their analogues in other cultures.

5.22 To judge from the examples considered in this paper, the figure of the trickster suggests the vulnerability of those in power. The stories considered can be read as reflections on the instability of this power. Possibly their telling is motivated by fear of losing this power. There is then an irony in the narratives: men are describing women who trick men.

5.3 The writings of structural anthropologists (Beidelman; Edwards; Lévi-Strauss) have much to say that is relevant to our discussion on how power politics is explored by the power brokers of ancient Israel. In essence, these scholars argue that folktales provide a means for exploring oppositions. Jay Edwards has summarized the matter in this way:

Because cognitively established binary oppositions (such as Life/Death, Male/Female, and Consanguinal Kin/Affinal Kin) cannot be easily resolved, the folktale provides a method of interrelating and mediating them. It performs the function of setting out an array of possibilities in narrative form for the appreciation of children and others. Folktales often deal with basic moral-philosophical dilemmas and the cultural norms for handling them. As T. D. Beidelman recently stated, trickster-based "anomalies serve didactically to stimulate . . . moral imagination so as to understand existential dilemmas which involve choice in conduct and ends" (1984:89).

5.4 In the biblical narratives considered in this study, role reversal occurs. Through trickery, by both women and men, the underdog plays the part of power broker and the one expected to wield authority is under the thumb of the weak. This analysis suggests that stories of the use of deception by one individual against another are concerned with the ambiguity of power and the social problem of order and disorder. The boundaries between those with legitimated authority and those deprived of it are blurred as the narratives comment on the seemingly fragile state of the social order.

6.1 To conclude, this paper began by considering the tendency of scholars to engage in cross-cultural comparison of trickster figures. Despite a few dissenting voices on this manner of doing research, most studies today are still exploring the analogues between these comical characters. The survey of the literature provided here and the comparison of Afro-American and African trickster stories to biblical stories of trickster figures suggest that the minority who advocate abandoning not only "trickster" as a technical term but also broad questions of cross-cultural functions of this character are moving in the right direction. Different types of trickster characters seem to be preferred in different cultures. Nevertheless, as a point of departure, the concept of trickster and a look at the cross-cultural evidence have been useful in illuminating a biblical phenomenon.

WORKS CONSULTED

Abrahams, Roger D.
    1975   "Negotiating Respect: Patterns of Presentation among Black Women." Pp. 58-80 in *Women and Folklore*. Ed. Claire R. Farrer. Austin: University of Texas Press.

Babcock-Abrahams, Barbara
    1975   "'A Tolerated Margin of Mess': The Trickster and His Tales Reconsidered." *Journal of the Folklore Institute* 11: 147-86.

Beidelman, T. D.
    1980   "The Moral Implications of the Kaguru: Some Thoughts on Tricksters, Translations and Comparative Analysis." *American Ethnologist* 7: 27-42.

Bremond, Claude
    1977   "The Morphology of the French Fairy Tale: The Ethical Model." Pp. 49-76 in *Patterns in Oral Literature*. Ed. Heda Jason and Dimitri Segal. Chicago: Aldine.

Brenner, Athalya
    1985   *The Israelite Woman*. Sheffield: JSOT Press.

Brinton, Daniel
    1868   *The Myths of the New World*. Philadelphia: David McKay.

Dance, Daryl C.
    1978   *Shuckin' and Jivin'*. Bloomington: Indiana University Press.

Draffkorn, Anne E.
    1957   "Ilâni/Elohim." *JBL* 76: 216-24.

Dundes, Alan
    1964   *The Morphology of North American Indian Tales*. Helsinki: Folklore Fellow Communications.

Edwards, Jay
    1978   *The Afro-American Trickster Tale: A Structural Analysis*. Bloomington: Indiana University Folklore Publications Group.
    1984   "Structural analysis of the Afro-American trickster tale." Pp. 81-103 in *Black Literature and Literary Theory*. Ed. Henry Louis Gates, Jr. New York: Methuen.

Evans-Pritchard, E. E., ed.
    1967   *The Zande Trickster*. Oxford: Clarendon Press.

Exum, J. Cheryl
    1983   "'You Shall Let Every Daughter Live': A Study of Exodus 1:8-2:10." *Semeia* 28: 63-82.

Genovese, Eugene D.
    1976   *Roll, Jordan, Roll*. New York: Vintage Books.

Good, Edwin M.
    1965   *Irony in the Old Testament*. Philadelphia: Westminster.

Greenberg, Moshe
    1962   "Another Look at Rachel's Theft of the Teraphim." *JBL* 81:239-48.

Grottanelli, Cristiano
    1983   "Tricksters, Scapegoats, Champions, Saviors." *History of Religions* 23: 117-39.

Jason, Heda
    1977   "A Model for Narrative Structure in Oral Literature." Pp. 99-140 in *Patterns in Oral Literature*. Ed. Heda Jason and Dimitri Segal. Chicago: Aldine.

Lévi-Strauss, Claude
    1958   *Structural Anthropology*. New York: Basic Books.
    1962   *The Savage Mind*. Chicago: University of Chicago Press.

Otwell, John H.
    1977   *And Sarah Laughed*. Philadelphia: Westminster.

Paulme, Denise
    1977   "Impossible Imitation in African Trickster Tales." Pp. 64-103 in *Forms of Folklore in Africa*. Ed. Bernth Lindfors. Austin: University of Texas Press.

Pedersen, Johannes
    1926   *Israel: Its Life and Culture*. Vol. 1. London: Oxford University.

Pelton, Robert D.
    1980   *The Trickster in West Africa: A Study of Mythic Irony and Sacred Delight*. Hermeneutics: Studies in the History of Religions. Berkeley: University of California.

von Rad, Gerhard
    1972   *Genesis*. Revised Edition. Old Testament Library. Philadelphia: Westminster.

Radin, Paul
    1972   *The Trickster*. New York: Schocken.

Smith, Michael G.
    1960   *Government in Zazzau, 1800-1950*. London: Oxford University.

Speiser, E. A.
    1964   *Genesis*. Anchor Bible, 1. Garden City, N.Y.: Doubleday.

Street, Bryan
    1972   "The Trickster Theme: Winnebago and Azande." Pp. 82-104 in *Zande Themes*. Ed. Andre Singer and Bryan Street. Oxford: Blackwell.

Wadlington, Warwick
    1975   *The Confidence Game in American Literature*. Princeton: Princeton University.

Weber, Max
    1947   *The Theory of Social and Economic Organization*. New York: Free Press.

Welsch, Roger L.
    1981   *Omaha Tribal Myths and Trickster Tales*. Chicago: Swallow Press.

Wertheim, Willem F.
  1965   "Society as a Composite of Conflicting Value Systems." Pp. 23-37 in *East-West Parallels*. Chicago: Quadrangle Books.
  1973   *Evolution or Revolution?* London: Pelican.
Westermann, Claus
  1985   *Genesis 12-36*. Minneapolis: Augsburg.

WISE AND STRANGE:
AN INTERPRETATION OF THE FEMALE IMAGERY
IN PROVERBS IN LIGHT OF TRICKSTER MYTHOLOGY

Claudia V. Camp
Texas Christian University

ABSTRACT

This article compares various manifestations of the trickster figure from comparative myth and folklore with the presentations of personified Wisdom and the Strange Woman in the book of Proverbs. There are five interrelated characteristics of the trickster that provide categories for analyzing these two female figures and their relationship to each other: the trickster's basic duality; the trickster's embrace of both order and disorder; the importance of language and the interconnection of wise and deceitful language; the problem of theodicy and the attempt to understand human evil; and the liminal status of the trickster. This reading of the female images in Proverbs through the lens of the trickster has the effect of undercutting the book's most obvious message of absolute opposition between good and evil as represented in the female figures, and highlighting their paradoxical, but experientially validated, unity. The paper concludes with reflections on the potential value of the "woman as trickster" image in feminist thought.

0.1 Cross-cultural studies have, in recent years, generated much enthusiasm among biblical scholars. They have been responded to with equally strong and well-taken words of caution about respect for cultural differences and for variations in apparent patterns of social behavior or mythological imagery. Nowhere is such caution more well-placed than in an attempt to identify elements of the trickster motif in a cultural tradition such as the Bible, which does not have any one character clearly identified as such, unlike the cycles of trickster stories that appear, for example, among many native North American tribes and also among certain African peoples (Thompson, Pelton). The Bible's lack of such a figure is only the first of several methodological difficulties that need at least an acknowledgement before one succumbs to the siren of comparison.

0.2   A second difficulty is that, even where comparative mythologists agree on the existence of a trickster, this figure is an extremely elusive and changeable one. What exactly makes a trickster a trickster? The trickster is often portrayed as an enormous buffoon who wanders the earth getting himself and others into trouble, largely because of his outlandish appetite for food and sex. Although he is called the trickster, as often as not he is more the fool, one who gets tricks played on him as well as tricking others. The trickster is a breaker of all social boundaries: not guided by any recognizable sense of good and evil, he flouts religious taboos and conventions of proper sexual behavior, even to the point of changing sex and becoming a man's "wife" for a period of time in one Winnebago episode (Radin: 22-24). In some folklore traditions, this radical "outside-the-normness" of the trickster results in his being cast as an animal rather than as a human, although always as an animal who interacts with other characters using the structures of human speech and society (even if only to abuse them).

0.21   Oddly, however (at least to the modern Western mind), trickster stories are not found threatening by their audiences but rather extremely humorous. Even more oddly, antics of this amoral buffoon are sometimes associated with the most serious tasks. Either an actual deity himself, or intimately associated with deity, the trickster regularly participates in the creation or transformation of the world, providing it with its basic cosmic and social structures, cultural knowledge, and deepest wisdom.

0.22   There does not seem to be any one "ideal" trickster type. Rather, any given trickster figure may comprise a shifting combination of several, but not necessarily all, characteristics of the general type. We may take some comfort, then, that one may analyze biblical texts under the aegis of the trickster mythologem without making absolute claims about whether a given character is or is not a trickster. The important task is to identify elements of the paradigm and examine how they function in relationship to each other and to other aspects of the culture (Pelton: 14-17). It is with such caution that I hope to treat the female imagery in Proverbs, where there are at least two major objections to finding a trickster. The most critical one is formal. These texts are not oral, folkloric narratives but literary, instructional poems. Second, and relatedly, they do not exhibit the non-judgmental hilarity that almost always characterizes trickster tales (though not always, as Pelton's presentation [164-222] of one West African trickster shows).

They are, rather, highly moralistic in tone and intent. Nonetheless, as I shall suggest, the presentation of the female figures in Prov 1-9 exhibits some striking similarities to the traditional trickster.

0.3 A third methodological problem lies not only in the diversity of the trickster, but also that of his interpreters. Anthropologists' treatments of the significance of the trickster have ranged from the psychic developmentalism of Radin and Jung to the mathematical structuralism of Lévi-Strauss. My own intellectual preference and, hence, the direction of this essay run toward the cultural hermeneutics approach of Robert Pelton. Unlike Radin and Jung, Pelton attempts to explain the often contradictory elements of the trickster myths holistically, rather than explaining them away in an evolutionary scheme that posits a development from animal to human, from amoral buffoon to a savior-transformer. Resisting Lévi-Strauss' tendency toward abstraction, Pelton insists on interpreting the trickster motifs with respect to their native cultural contexts. One may generalize about the trickster as a combination liar, buffoon, and culture-hero, but these traits are always narratively manifest in culturally specific ways that enable a given culture to interpret itself to itself. This concern for cultural specificity built into a comparative method is, at the very least, reassuring and, at best, should enable us to deepen our understanding of Israel's efforts to interpret its own situation.

0.4 Finally, we must take consideration of the fact that the biblical figures to whom I wish to apply the trickster paradigm are female, rather than male, which makes them unique in any comparative studies with which I am familiar.[1] The significance of this fact is open to question. We must recognize, first of all, that trickster mythology can be applied to male as well as to female characters in the Bible. Jacob, for instance, would be a prime candidate. Thus, the Bible does not simply reverse the typical expectations. Nonetheless, as other essays in this volume show, the Bible does have a tradition of "tricky" or deceitful women that should tell us something about Israel's understanding of itself and its women (cf. Camp: 124-40). Furthermore, the trickster is often portrayed as an animal, a being on the boundary between the human and the natural worlds. S. Ortner has demonstrated a certain proclivity to relate "female" to "nature" in contrast to the connection of "male" with "culture." Her analysis raises the possibility that female imagery, in characters exhibiting other elements of the trickster pattern, functions similarly to the theriomorphism of other tricksters.

---

[1] I would like to thank Carole Fontaine for stressing this distinction to me in personal communication.

0.5 While attempting to bear these cautionary notes in mind, it will be the thesis of this paper that a comparison of various manifestations of the trickster figure from comparative myth and folklore with the presentations of personified Wisdom and the Strange Woman in the book of Proverbs provides useful interpretive insights into the biblical material. Moreover, this comparison is informative not only at the several points where biblical female imagery fits the typical trickster model, but also where it does not. There are five interrelated characteristics of the trickster that provide categories for analyzing personified Wisdom, the Strange Woman, and their relationship to each other.

1. Duality

1.1 The first and most all-embracing of these characteristics, recognized by virtually all commentators, is the basic duality of the trickster. Reading through the collection of any given society's trickster tales, one always finds not only the fooler, but also the fool, both a creator and a disrupter of order. The female imagery in Proverbs also plays upon opposites, personified Wisdom representing creation, love, life, truth, social order and wisdom, while the Strange Woman represents death, falsehood, social disruption and folly. The concern for the proper boundaries of sexual behavior, flaunted so gleefully by the trickster, is also quite evident in Proverbs. Female Wisdom is associated with the wife whom one is to love faithfully (4:6; 5:15-19; 7:4; 8:17), while the Strange Woman allures with provocative descriptions of illicit sex (7:10-20).

1.2 The relationship of the positive and negative elements of the trickster has been a subject of debate among anthropologists. Paul Radin argues, for example, based on certain native American cycles, that the connection of the trickster with cosmogonic activity is a secondary accretion to the trickster mythology, a position which seems to have a fair amount of textual support in the traditions he studied (124-31; 155-69). Much more speculative, and also suspect because of its evolutionary presupposition, is his assertion that the trickster's "culture-hero" traits—the various ways he orders or initiates important social structures or useful cultural objects—are later "developments" from an "original" conception of a primordial person obsessed by hunger, wanderlust, and sexuality, purposeless and little differentiated from the animal world (165-68). Radin suggests that the elevation of the trickster to divine status with a role in creation was the work of an ancient "priest-thinker" trying to assimilate the even older myths into an aboriginal theological system (164).

1.21 Unfortunately, this postulated evolution of the trickster literature does not explain the persistent attractiveness of the figure in his dual roles. Pelton's project takes on this issue with the assumption that members of pre-modern societies sought after a unity of experience in their lives and mythologies and, therefore, that the interpreter "can best approach the many aspects of pre-modern religious life by searching for the logic that knits diversity together" (11). I should make clear that Pelton does not imply any particular form of modern logic in this statement. The questions, rather, are those of how any given society structures the diverse and sometimes contradictory elements of the trickster pattern, how these elements work in relation to each other and to other social structures, and thus, how that society uses the trickster to uncover and interpret the meaning of its life and world (16).

1.22   Unlike the trickster who unites this duality into a single paradoxical entity, the female characterization in Proverbs divides it into two distinct figures. These opposites nonetheless "attract." J.-N. Aletti has noted with particular astuteness the many connecting links between the positive and negative female imagery in chs. 1-9. He argues that the editor of this material has created a very deliberate confusion between Wisdom and the Strange Woman through the ambiguous use of certain vocabulary (1977: 132-34). Prov 4:8 assures the young man that Wisdom will honor him if he *embraces* (חבק) her, while 5:20 questions why he would *embrace* (חבק) the bosom of the Strange Woman. Even more emphatically, one must *grasp* (חזק) Wisdom and Instruction (3:18; 4:13) and expect to be *grasped* (חזק) by the Strange Woman (7:13). All this grasping and grabbing will take place "in the street" and "in the marketplace" where *both* Wisdom and the Strange Woman are to be found (1:20-21; 7:12). After the encounter in the public place, both female figures invite the listener to their respective houses (the Strange Woman's or Folly's in 7:15-20 and 9:14-16; Wisdom's in 8:34 and 9:1-6). Both Wisdom and Folly offer *bread* (לחם) at their banquets (9:5, 17). The imagery of water is used to allure the young man to his own wife:

> Drink water from your own cistern,
> flowing water from your own well (5:15);

as well as to seduce him to Folly's house:

> Stolen water is sweet,
> and bread eaten in secret is pleasant (9:17).

With either the Strange Woman or his wife, he can *fill himself* (רוה) with *love* (דדים, 7:18) or *breasts* (דַּדֶּיהָ-, 5:19, perhaps a scribal error, but carrying the same implications!). Finally, the word used to describe the truthful teaching of the sage (לקח) is the same as that employed for the seductive speech of the Strange Woman who is said to be "wily of heart" (1:5; 4:2; 9:9; 7:21).

1.3 Comparison with the trickster invites the interpreter of Proverbs to take seriously the literary unity of the Strange Woman and personified Wisdom before separating them too quickly into "good" and "evil." I have suggested elsewhere that other biblical imagery for women points in this same direction. Like the trickster and the Strange Woman—and indeed, by association, like Wisdom herself (Camp: 129-33)—Tamar (Gen 38), Ruth, and Judith all break their society's boundaries on sexual behavior in order to accomplish good for themselves, for society, and, ultimately, for Yhwh (cf. Craven). Like the trickster also, Tamar and Ruth, in particular, undertake their risky strategies primarily out of their own self-interest. Only secondarily and unintentionally do their actions benefit the larger group (cf. Radin: 125). Yet the biblical authors, like the tricksters' tradents, understand the women's intentions and their effects as of one piece.

1.31 This subtle underlying unity of personified Wisdom and the Strange Woman provides a counterweight to the more polemical overtones of ancient instruction ("Understand, my son, that there are two distinct groups of women in the world . . .") and modern critique ("Look, my daughter, how men have divided us into virgins and whores . . ."). Such a perspective allows an interpretation of female Wisdom and the Strange Woman not along traditional patriarchal lines of "virgin versus whore" or "the ideal woman on a pedestal versus the degraded woman of male experience," but rather as a representation of the necessary complementarity of human experience. If Israel, in splitting the typical paradoxically single trickster, has to some degree denied rather than affirmed this complementarity, we now at least have a basis for a specific and constructive critique that goes beyond the limitations of a polemic against patriarchy in general (cf. Johanson's admonition to take on this task). The remaining sections of this essay will address some of the different aspects of this fundamental feature of duality. In particular, an issue that emerges in the Proverbs material is that of how Israel has here structured its experience of the conjunction, as well as the opposition, of good and evil, and what role female imagery has played in that structuring.

2. *Order and Disorder*
2.1 As we have already noted, the trickster represents the forces of creation and destruction, order and disorder, on both the cosmic and social levels. Although the temptation here, once again, is to see two "originally" distinct characters at work, the structure of many trickster episodes reveals the inherent unity of these two movements. Raven, the

North American Haida trickster, for example, begins his creative work by skinning a newborn child and appropriating its skin for himself, and then stealing and eating people's eyeballs (Radin: 156-58)! Similarly, the trickster's introduction of valuable tools or social customs to a society often takes place without any intentionality on his part and, indeed, often as the result of some otherwise unpleasant trick he has played on someone (Radin: 125). Occasionally, this intermixture of ordering and disordering activities results in an ironic double paradox, as in one of Pelton's parade examples, the conflict between Ananse, the trickster of the West African Ashante tribe and the misanthropic character, Hate-to-be-contradicted (25-27). Hate-to-be-contradicted lives on the outskirts of society and fools visitors into contradicting him by telling outlandish stories, and then kills them. Hate-to-be-contradicted is outdone by his own contradiction of the even wilder lies told by Ananse, who then takes license to kill him. Having performed this apparent favor for society, however, Ananse cuts his antagonist into bits and "sows" contradiction among humans!

2.11 Contrary, perhaps, to our expectations, the Ashante do not condemn Ananse for his introduction of contradiction into human discourse, but rather delight in this expression of what they know to be their reality. In this, as in other stories, the trickster embraces and embodies the paradox of order and disorder (Pelton: 29).

> Disorder belongs to the totality of life, and the spirit of this disorder is the Trickster. His function . . . is to add disorder to order and so make a whole, to render possible, within the bounds of what is permitted, an experience of what is not permitted (Kerenyi: 185).

The important point is that the forces of disorder are brought inside human territory. Ananse and Hate-to-be-contradicted behave in virtually the same manner, except for the fact that the latter refuses human intercourse while the former insists on it, even in its negativity. "The true limen," suggests Pelton, "lies not on or outside the margins of society, but in its midst" (37).

2.2 That personified Wisdom and the Strange Woman represent forces of order and disorder is abundantly clear. Wisdom participates in the ordering process of Yhwh's creation (8:22-31) and is responsible for the governance of society (8:15-16) and the well-being of her followers (8:18, 35-36). The doubled epithet repeatedly applied to the negative female figure—strange woman, foreign woman—captures in its very ambiguity the multi-leveled nature of the threat she presents to the orders of life and society (Camp: 115-20). She guards the gateway to death (2:18-39; 9:18), countering Wisdom's offer of life. This death, though imaged in virtually mythological terms, has a concrete social form: being "cut off from the land" (2:22) and descending to "the point of utter ruin in the assembled congregation" (5:14). Clearly, the community feels a threat to itself in the actions of the individual.

2.3 For all these obvious oppositions between the ordering of Woman Wisdom and the disordering of the Strange Woman, the trickster paradigm invites us to consider the intersections of these forces as well. The Strange Woman, in spite of her "foreignness," exists very much within the boundaries of society. She appears in the public places of the community and invites people to her house, just as Woman Wisdom does. In portraying the Strange Woman in this manner, the Israelite sages have not excluded foreignness, but, in fact, let it "in." In so doing, they have acknowledged the reality that a system of order cannot afford to exclude anomaly without ultimately being overwhelmed by it (Pelton: 251). Here the apparently negative Strange Woman enacts one of the paradoxically positive roles of the trickster, symbolizing the manner in which people try to integrate disorder, the anomalous, into their daily lives.

2.31 The house and paths of the Strange Woman, moreover, bring within the boundaries of Israel's communal apprehension the ultimate disorder, namely, death. Trickster figures are often credited with bringing death into human existence and, thereby, capturing death's "centripetality" for the center of life and guaranteeing life's "eternal reirruption" (Pelton: 263; cf. Radin: 147). If this evaluation of death seems a bit *too* positive with respect to Proverbs, we ought nonetheless to remember that the "first woman," Eve, accepted death as the price of a fully human life. The entry of death into human life through the mediation of the woman and the serpent (certainly another trickster figure!) goes hand in hand with the acquisition of knowledge of good and evil which, for the sage, means life. At the heart of wisdom thought, then, lies the trickster's paradox: death does yield life. (See below for further consideration of the Eden story.)

2.32 Death as a metaphor in Prov 1-9 may be less focussed on biological death than on the related connotations of separation from deity and community, perhaps more terrifying ideas to Israel (cf. Bailey: 41). If we assume that the book of Proverbs became prominent religious literature after the Exile, Israel's experience of communal "death" in Babylon (Ezek 37:1-14) and their subsequent struggle to maintain an identifiable community in post-exilic Judah may also be reflected in this material. In that case the acknowledgment of the Strange Woman, with all her danger, inside the community's boundaries becomes all the more striking. And, in spite of the danger, this acknowledgment is quite complete, as witnessed by the poem in Prov 7, which paints a shameless picture of her attractions (vv. 13-20) before warning of her consequences. Knowledge of evil must accompany knowledge of good in the search for wisdom and life. Without an appreciation for the strange, a society does not know its own boundaries.

2.4 To complete the paradox of order and disorder encompassed by the female imagery in Proverbs, we must recognize not only the Strange Woman's *inclusion* within Israel's social boundaries, but also personified Wisdom's *transgression* of them. She is, first of all, one of the most universal, non-xenophobic images in the Hebrew Bible, comparable in this respect to Second Isaiah's Servant. She crosses, moreover, the most fundamental line of all, that between creator and created, and in both directions, as is typical of tricksters. She is at one and the same time human wisdom elevated to the word of God (witness the canonical status of Proverbs) and divine wisdom come to reside among humans. But, contrary to expectations, her elevation does not result in death (contrast the king of Tyre, Ezek 28), nor is her "descent" from heaven the result of anything other than her own initiative (Prov 8:30-31). The boundary-crossing which ought to destroy instead becomes a source of life, but we can see the true value of this life only if we also recognize the dangerously disordering process through which it becomes available.

3. Language of Wisdom and Deceit

3.1 Pelton argues that the bringing of reality to language and the definition of human being as being engaged in discourse, usually accomplished through foolishness or deceit, is one of the hallmarks of the trickster. "The trickster brings to light all non-sense so that all might become language and therefore human" (242).

3.11 The Ashante's Ananse provides a variety of amusing examples. In addition to introducing contradiction into human discourse, Ananse also saves speech for human beings by tricking a monster bird into returning the jaws he stole from human faces (40). He is also associated with the spread of wisdom, which he initially tries to hide by putting it in a gourd at the top of a tree. Aggravated because his son can climb the tree better than he, however, he breaks the gourd and hurls its contents to the earth. In a wonderfully complex episode, Ananse helps the Sun assume his rightful position as High God in the pantheon and settler of human disputes, but again by trickery. He steals a certain word from the Creator God that Sun must know in order to prove his worthiness for the position, and then aids Sun's memory of it by fashioning a drum whose resonance imitates the sound of the word. Pelton comments that the "light" needed to fashion order out of the tangle of human wills can only be focussed through a duplicity that restarts the processes of speech.... Ananse rejects truth in favor of lying, but only for the sake of speech... (50-51).

Furthermore, as a reward for his success in this episode, Ananse's name is given to all the stories—*anansesem*—through which the Ashante remember and shape their culture (27-31, 224).

3.12   These Ashante tales represent only a few of the episodes associating various West African tricksters with language. Compare also Pelton's discussions of the Fon's Legba, the "divine linguist" (72); the Yoruba's Eshu, the introducer of divination (133-48); or the Dogon's Ogo-Yurugu who, with his twin, possesses the forty-eight categories into which the Dogon divide all speech (188-89).

3.2   The connections of personified Wisdom and the Strange Woman to language are numerous and, again, more subtle and complex than might appear at first glance. Woman Wisdom announces herself as a speaker of truth and a hater of perverted speech (8:6-9, 13). Her instruction brings happiness and life (8:32-35). The invitations of the Strange Woman (or Woman Folly in 9:13) are, of course, understood as seductions that lead to death. We must, however, consider the underlying currents that partially blur this surface opposition.

3.3   Like Ananse, Woman Wisdom presides over and authorizes a tradition (Gilbert: 218; Lang: 170-71) that is terribly concerned with language and its proper use. The basic values as represented in the proverb collections are to speak as little as possible (10:19; 13:3; 17:25; 29:20; *passim*), as effectively as possible (15:23; 25:11,15; *passim*), and to recognize that no matter what one says, Yhwh may have something else in mind (21:1,2; 20:21; *passim*). Righteous speech is also of great importance (10:11,20,21,31,32; *passim*), but it shares center stage with words fitly or efficaciously spoken. The moral value of proverbial language is occasionally ambiguous, moreover. The observation that "a bribe is a magic stone in the eye of him who gives it" (17:8) creates almost as much temptation as the description of the Strange Woman in Prov 7. Finally, proverbs that counsel opposite courses of action (presumably depending on the situation; cf. 26:4,5) indicate an awareness that this form of commonsense truth is to some degree relative and immethodical (cf. Geertz: 23-24). The tradition personified by Woman Wisdom recognizes, then, a complexity in human existence and in the speech which articulates it.

3.4   A similar ambiguity exists in the proverb collection with respect to the relationship of folly and wickedness. Although both are evaluated negatively, folly does not entail the dire consequences associated with Woman Folly in 9:13, who opens the same doorway to death as does the Strange Woman in other poems. R. B. Y. Scott has noted that the contrasted pairs of righteousness and wickedness, on the one hand, and wisdom and folly, on the other, are not interchangeable in the collection (153-54). The fool can expect poverty and disrepute, but this does not carry an explicitly religious value judgment with it (ibid: 158). Frequently, the actions of fools are simply described (12:15,23; 13:16; 15:21; 18:2) as if no further comment were necessary, and folly is considered its own reward (16:22). The warnings against the consequences of folly, both to the fool and to others, are sometimes couched in images that border on the amusing and, indeed, remind us of the trickster.

> Like one who binds the stone in the sling
> is the one who gives honor to a fool (26:8).
>
> Like a dog that returns to his vomit
> is a fool that repeats his folly (26:11).

The sluggard, in particular, is depicted in laughable images (22:13; 26:13,14,15), and there is one character who is even worse than the fool:

> Do you see a man who is wise in his own eyes?
> There is more hope for a fool than for him (26:12).

3.5 Although this nuance and complexity found in the tradition is seemingly reduced by the either-or opposition of Woman Wisdom and the Strange Woman in the poems of chs. 1-9, even here the matter is not quite so simple. As Aletti's analysis pointed out (see above), the one who wishes to distinguish between these two female figures must first contend with their similarities. Aletti argues further that this potential confusion of values was quite intentional on the part of the sage, who used it as one means of emphasizing the crucial importance of language to society as a whole and in the endeavors of the wisdom tradition in particular and, for these very reasons, the dangers of its abuse (139-40).

3.51 The crowning irony in this nexus of language, wisdom, and deceit comes in Prov 18:21, which introduces yet another female image, "Lady Tongue" (Williams: 91).

> Death and Life are in the hand of the tongue,
> and her lovers will eat of her fruit.

Those who are lovers of language, and the sages are most certainly among them, can expect to taste the fruits of both the Strange Woman's deceit, namely death, and Woman Wisdom's truth, the life that comes from Yhwh (8:35). The fundamental duality that exists in human intercourse is inescapable. Language may, in the abstract, separate truth and deceit, but in experience the two often become one.

3.6 This duality is often treated elsewhere in the Bible with greater appreciation and, sometimes, humor than it is in Prov 1-9. This is nowhere more true than in stories of some of the female characters who are related in theme and imagery to personified Wisdom and the Strange Woman (Camp: 124-40). I have already alluded to the social boundary-defying sexual activity of Tamar, Ruth, and Judith. In this context, we need also note that the ploys of Tamar and Judith are accompanied by deceitful speech, as is also true in Rebekah's scheme to win the first-born's blessing for Jacob (Gen 27). Esther provides another example of cagey locution and circumlocution which, while not quite deceitful, was, at the appropriate moments, less than completely straightforward (cf. Talmon: 437). Finally, in yet another twist on truth, deceit, and their anticipated consequences, the wise (but calculating) Abigail kills her husband Nabal (whose name means "the fool") with the absolute, unvarnished truth (1 Sam 25:37-38)!

4. Theodicy

4.1 Although I have yet to see the word "theodicy" used by anthropologists in their studies of tricksters, it should be clear from the themes of order and disorder, truth and falsehood which we have already discussed that the question of good and evil, and their relationship to the deity, cannot lurk far in the background. We have seen enough of the trickster to know that, in him, various cultural understandings of good and evil merge in complex ways. What is less obvious, and, indeed, varies from culture to culture, is the role of the deity in all of this. Sometimes the trickster *is* a deity who represents a primordial blend of power, creativity, and destructiveness, for example, the Haida's Raven (see above; Radin: 156-58). Other times, he is a being created by the High God for a special purpose. In an episode of the Winnebago trickster mythology, Earthmaker tellls the trickster, Wakdjunkaga

> Firstborn, you are the oldest of all those I have created. I created you good-natured: I made you a sacred person. I sent you to the earth to remain there so that human beings would listen to you, honor you and obey you and that you might teach them by what means they could secure a happy life . . . (Radin: 150).

Earthmaker goes on to chastise Wakdjunkaga gently for bringing trouble on himself by making light of the deity's creation. Radin notes, however, that even within one tradition, interpretations of the trickster can vary. By the early twentieth century, some Winnebagos influenced by syncretized Christian beliefs had moralized the trickster stories as examples of inappropriate behavior, or even equated him with Satan (148-50).

4.11   The pattern varies again in the case of Ogo-Yurugu, the trickster of the West African Dogon tribe. In Dogon mythology, Ogo-Yurugu is one of a set of primordial twins who rebels against the High God, Amma, his creator, because of his fear that Amma would deny him a mate. Although Ogo-Yurugu is finally defeated by Amma and banished from the divine and human domains (he becomes a fox), his attempts to wrest control from Amma result in the shape of the world as the Dogon know it.

> [T]he Dogon too must cope with solitude, sexual anxiety and death. They do not, however, look at these experiences or the rebellion that caused them as unequivocally evil. Without Ogo's search for his female twin nothing would be what it is, and even as Yurugu [the fox], he continues to reveal and enlarge the boundaries of life. The "beneficent ferment" of Ogo's opposition complements the orderly graciousness of Amma (Pelton: 207).

4.2   The Judeo-Christian reader of the Wakdjunkaga and Ogo-Yurugu stories is inevitably tempted to make comparisons with the biblical story of creation and "fall." This placement of the trickster in the role of the archetypal human would not be altogether inaccurate. Over and over his interpreters comment that the trickster's role is that of making the human world human. The questions raised by this mythology for the biblical tradition are: how evil is evil, and what does God have to do with this dimension of human experience?

4.21   According to one interpretive stance, the negative aspects of the human condition are punishment for the sin of disobedience to God, enacted out of human free will and thus absolving God of responsibility in the matter. Although on one level, such an interpretation seems comparable to the trickster stories of rebellion against, or at least carelessness of, the High God's purposes, it does not cope well with their lightness, humor, and irony, and their acceptance of human "evil." Nor does such a position deal well with certain intra-biblical dilemmas, for example, the terrible logical problem of the existence of evil under the reign of a good and all-powerful God, or the occasional biblical revelation of God's maleficence (especially in Job and Qoheleth).

4.22   The trickster stories represent a different approach to the problem of evil. This approach is more descriptive (being often etiological) than prescriptive, and it is less concerned with explaining evil than it is with interpreting the human condition of which evil is a part. The paradoxical unity of good and evil in the trickster is basically a manifestation of the way human life is. This approach also, then, begs the metaphysical question of the relationship of a good God to evil, but it does recognize the reality of a human experience of evil which is not explicable in the terms of a simplistic theory of retribution. In many respects, I would suggest, the commonsense, human-oriented attitude to this issue found in the trickster stories is most closely akin to that expressed in biblical material associated with wisdom.[2]

4.3 We have already noted some of the moral ambiguities in the proverb collection. This ambiguity is coupled with variant evaluations of vocabulary associated with wisdom, both within Proverbs itself (McKane: 10-22) and elsewhere as, for example, in the Succession Narrative (Whybray: 57-9). Nowhere is this more clear than in the Eden story, where the crafty (ערום)[3] serpent leads the way to both human mortality and wisdom. In addition to the traditional interpretation of this story as one of sin and punishment, G. Mendenhall has also found here a scathing critique of wisdom. I am not convinced that either of these perspectives is completely correct.

4.31 The simplistic notion of sin and punishment does not deal with the complexities of the text, both in what it does and does not say. First, it does not deal with God's ultimate responsibility for the situation. Who, after all, created the serpent and his intellectual abilities, and provided the temptation of a forbidden tree? The Eden story is really quite like a trickster tale in this respect, concerned not with explaining or rationalizing every logical possibility of a situation but rather with enfolding in an imaginative, narrative embrace the "way things are" for human beings, in other words, with describing and interpreting the human condition. The text is curiously silent about Yhwh's emotions in reaction to the human deed, especially with regard to any "wrath" one might expect the deity to feel. Yhwh simply asks what has occurred (3:11,13), describes what every Israelite knows to be the nature of existence (3:14-19), and then makes clothes for the man and woman (3:21). The work of P. Trible on the literary features of this material and C. Meyers on its sociological context makes abundantly clear both the descriptive, rather than prescriptive, nature of the text, and its concern to bring meaning (not merely condemnation) to the brokenness of human life.

---

[2] I recognize the difficulties in defining "wisdom literature" or the "wisdom tradition" in the Bible. For our present purposes, we need no more precision than that of broad similarities of vocabulary and theme.
[3] Compare the positive evaluations of this word in Prov 12:3; 13:16; 14:14; *passim*.

> The elementary questions about life and its hardships, about the endless and excessive efforts to survive—these are the human enigmas of existence to which this passage speaks. The gnawing WHY—why is life so hard for both men and women, why is there so much to be done for survival alone—is dealt with here (Meyers: 348).

The answer? Simply that "the human condition is ordained by God and must be accepted as such" (ibid.: 348-49).

4.32 Is, then, Gen 2-3 a condemnation of human wisdom? It is true that wisdom that is "wise in its own eyes" and that does not allow for the disposing of Yhwh as well as the proposing of human beings is condemned by the sages, not only in the critical books of Job and Qoheleth but also in that bastion of human optimism, Proverbs itself. The universality of this critique in the wisdom tradition suggests to me that Mendenhall's interpretation is off-target and that, once again, Genesis' intent is to understand, not condemn, human reality as the author knows it. Yes, the Eden story does associate the acquisition of human wisdom with death, but the rest of the Hebrew Bible makes clear that the mere fact of human mortality is not overly troubling to the ancient Israelites (Bailey: 47-57). Death, too, is part of the "way life is." More importantly, I think, Gen 3 reveals that wisdom, like death—and also like the hard work of farming, the bearing of children, the wearing of clothes, and so on—is part of *human* life.

4.4 The wisdom tradition was willing both to exalt and to criticize itself, but both evaluations were made from the perspective of human beings. Even the God of the whirlwind who appears in Job, I would argue, is a God poetically articulated from a consciously human experience, with no pretense of recording direct divine revelation. The wisdom tradition articulates various facets of the interface between an ambiguous human wisdom and a God who should be good and just, but who is not always so experienced. Wisdom *is* theodicy, not conceived as a metaphysical problem, but experienced in the way we live.

4.41 Woman Wisdom and the Strange Woman in Proverbs also speak to this condition, as always, paradoxically. On the one hand, they represent the idealized conceptualization of good and evil: ever separate, with ever inevitable consequences. Under the surface, however, as Aletti's analysis makes clear, lurks the dangerous knowledge that life does not always work so neatly. The Strange Woman is such a horror because her words are so close to the truth, not the truth of tidy theological packages, but the truth as humans really experience it. Husbands do go away on business, and strange beds do offer delight.

The depth of the paradox only becomes visible when we acknowledge the unity of the female imagery that embraces the duality. In their embodiment, Woman Wisdom and the Strange Woman are one, a fact that the sages' evaluations of them (e.g., 7:4-5) only partially mitigate. As woman, her dual path runs from heaven to Sheol and back, never failing to pass through human territory. The unity of the imagery is important for the same reason the trickster is important. It is a way of representing, and thus encompassing, the anomaly that exists in human life.

4.42 The female imagery does not, then, simply mediate between the human and the divine, as I have previously suggested (Camp: 272-81), or only between human life and death (see above), but also unites divinity with death. In the connection of this imagery *both* to Yhwh *and* Sheol, the full range of human experience of anomaly is incorporated, not only that of the material and social world, but that of the spirit as well. The ambiguity of the female imagery reflects the moral ambiguity of the deity which stands in the shadows of Eden and bursts forth in the Joban whirlwind. It thereby acknowledges what all humans experientially know: we cannot receive good from the hand of Yhwh and not receive evil also (cf. Job 2:10).

4.43 The unity of this imagery brings a new meaning to death as well. If the woman whose dwelling place is in Sheol is, on one level, the same as she who plays before Yhwh, and if this woman is the human reflection of the nature of God, then God's presence in Sheol is also affirmed. This theological perception is rare in the Bible (cf. Ps 139:8); it is typically either denied (Job 7:21; Ps 88:3-5,10-12 [H:4-6,11-13]; Isa 38:18-19) or, in the case of Job, tantalizingly tasted (15:13; 28:22). In Proverbs, by means of the female imagery, the chaotic anomaly of death is brought fully within the compass not only of human but also of divine experience. The female imagery in Proverbs anticipates the Gospel of John in more ways than one! The words of Pelton regarding the trickster may be accurately applied, *mutatis mutandis*, to the Strange Woman and Woman Wisdom.

> [The trickster] affirms the doubleness of the real and denies every one dimensional image of it. If he struggles with the High God and causes pain and death to enter the world, spoiling primordial bliss, his quarrel is not with the divine order as such, but with a false human image of the sacred, one that cannot encompass suffering, disorder, and the ultimate mess of death (262-63).

No less than Job, although through very different literary means, do the women of Proverbs participate in this struggle.

5. Liminality

5.1 The notion of liminality is derived by its greatest conceptualist, Victor Turner, from the middle phase of the rite of passage described by A. van Gennep. The first phase involves separation "from an earlier fixed point in the social structure, from a set of cultural conditions . . ., or from both." Then,

> during the intervening liminal period, the characteristics of the ritual subject . . . are ambiguous: he passes through a cultural realm that has few or none of the attributes of the past or coming state.

Finally, the person is reincorporated into a stable, but new, social or cultural state (94-95). It is the middle phase that is of concern here.

> Liminal entities are neither here nor there; they are betwixt and between the positions assigned and arrayed by law, custom, convention, and ceremonial. As such, their ambiguous and indeterminate attributes are expressed by a rich variety of symbols in the many societies that ritualize social and cultural transitions. Thus, liminality is frequently likened to death, to being in the womb, to invisibility, to darkness, to bisexuality, to the wilderness, and to an eclipse of the sun or moon (95).

5.11 Turner does not limit his concept of liminality to ritual passage, however, but rather applies it to any "anti-structural" person, group, condition, or cultural form that marks a transition from old to new (108-13). One common denominator is the social recognition that liminality involves *danger* to the social order, but that this danger must be accepted if the order is to sustain continued life. It is this broad use of the term that is employed by Pelton to understand many dimensions of the trickster tales. One of these, the inclusion of disorder within the boundaries of order, has already received attention in our discussion. Two others deserve consideration: the imaging of the trickster in animal forms (and the attendant question of the significance of the female imagery in Proverbs) and the mediation of the trickster between the realms of the sacred and daily life.

5.2 The connection of liminality with nature is articulated by Turner.

> Since liminality represents what Erving Goffman would call a "leveling and stripping" of structural status, an important component of the liminal situation is . . . an enhanced stress on "nature" at the expense of culture. Not only does it represent a situation of instruction . . . but it is also replete with symbols quite explicitly relating to biological processes, human and non-

human, and to other aspects of the natural order. In a sense, when man ceases to be the master and becomes the equal or fellow of man, he also ceases to be the master and becomes the equal or fellow of non-human beings ("Passages, Margins, and Poverty: Religious Symbols of Communitas," *Worship* 46 (1972): 410; quoted by Pelton: 34).

Based on this analysis, Pelton argues quite effectively that, where animal imagery is used of tricksters, it is essential to their structure and is, indeed, a source of their transforming power, for the liminal state is the source of personal and social regeneration (34-35).

5.21 The fascinating but difficult question we must address here is whether the female imagery in Proverbs serves the same function as the theriomorphism in the typical trickster pattern. Ortner's provocative theoretical analysis of female subordination based on women's association with nature would certainly point in that direction. How such a theoretical generalization might work itself out in Israel and, specifically, in the book of Proverbs, remains to be seen.

5.22 Although one may well debate Ortner's conclusion that woman's perceived "closeness" to nature is *the* fundamental cause of female subordination, it is certainly the case that in ancient Israel, as in virtually all known societies, women were subordinate. The question, then, becomes, whether this "less-than-male" status has a hermeneutical function in Proverbs similar to the trickster's liminal animality. I would suggest that it does and that this function finds its focus in the poems' representation of woman as the source of both power and love. Such a representation is "anti-structure" at its most apparent. Typically, in Israel, the source of power and love would have been Yhwh, usually imaged as male, mediated through the male power structures of society. The depiction of a woman in these roles is, then, the antithesis not only of the normal social order but of the normal theological order as well. Woman's role itself is transformed in Proverbs: she is the source of the community's life not in the usual biological sense of childbearer ("nature"), but in the socio-cultural and religious domains.

5.23 Although a liminal entity or state represents "anti-structure" in Turner's conceptualization, this anti-structure is understood by society to reveal its deeper identity and serve as a regenerating force. Turner cites studies by anthropologist M. Fortes suggesting that

> where patrilineality is the basis of social structure, an individual's link to other members of society through the mother, and hence by extension and abstraction "women" and "femininity," tends

> to symbolize that wider community and its ethical system that encompasses and pervades the politico-legal system (117).

I have argued elsewhere that personified Wisdom and the Strange Woman in the post-exilic period seem to embody just such a dynamic (Camp: 261-81). At a time when the center of male power, the monarchy, had been eradicated, the kind of power born of the love and nurture of the woman-centered family household recalls Israel to its fundamental values and serves as the life-and identity-source for the community.

5.3 A second dimension of liminality evident in the trickster is that of his movement and mediation between the world of the sacred and that of daily life. Liminality is not a static position, but a passageway between one condition and another, a process that transforms one state into a new one. The trickster is, at one and the same time, non-human, human, and beyond-the-human.

> [A]s the master of all language, he is . . . the meeting-place of all worlds. If, then, he is the image of the ironically imaginative mind of man, he is equally the image of the adaptability of transcendence, for which no material thing is too trivial to become a hierophany, not even that little gust of tongue-shaped breath known as the human word (Pelton: 269).

In all of Israel's religious literature, it is the wisdom tradition that most clearly discloses such a meeting place of the divine and the human. Here, the sacred is not set apart in the holy of holies, or reserved for the chosen few prophets. Woman Wisdom, who embodies both human wisdom and divine authority in an unexpected female form, stands in the public places, calling to and delighting in all בני אדם. J. Williams has argued that woman and the feminine in Israelite tradition often symbolize the boundary-dwelling of Israel and its God (127-30; *passim*). Female imagery for Wisdom, then, reinforces this paradoxically liminal dimension of the tradition that yet exists in the midst of things. There is indeed a sense in which the wisdom tradition is, as its scholarly denigrators have long argued, set apart from "mainstream Yahwism." What the trickster paradigm makes clear is that Yahwism could not long exist without it.

6. Conclusion and Feminist Reflections

6.1 In the foregoing discussion, I have employed the trickster pattern well-known in world mythology as a hermeneutical resource for analyzing the female imagery in Proverbs. Although I doubt that a folklorist or a biblical scholar would conclusively agree that this double female figure is in fact a true trickster, I have argued that the abundant points of connection afford the trickster paradigm some interpretive value with respect to personified Wisdom and the Strange Woman. To generalize, we might say that reading Prov 1-9 through the lens of the trickster produces a form of deconstructive reading of the text, undercutting its most obvious message of absolute opposition between good and evil as represented in these two figures, and highlighting their paradoxical, but experientially validated, unity.

6.2 From the perspective of feminist critique and theology, this paradox persists. In Proverbs, we are met first by a strong, exalted, almost deified female figure in personified Wisdom, surely the apex of biblical female imagery. On the other hand, we confront her opposite, the Strange Woman, and begin to fear that, once again, images of women are being used by men to support their own place of power in the social structure and the view of reality that supports it. The trickster paradigm opens yet a third possibility: a positive valuation of women's power as anti-structural, regenerative because of its liminality. But again we face paradox: what structures are being regenerated by this liminality? Is it all too convenient for the patriarchal power structure to give liminality its due in order to draw on its power for themselves?

6.21 The reality is that all of these various forces are at work in the mix of human life, which is one reason why feminists may choose different, but equally valid, courses of resistance to the patriarchal system. Some choose to separate themselves, to live on the margins of patriarchy. This is fine, as long as it is recognized that, by removing liminality from the center of the world, one abdicates the power to transform the world. But perhaps a new world is possible. Others choose to work within the system. This again is a valid choice, but only paradoxically so: the power that might transform the world also helps to support its present form. But perhaps the gain will outweigh the loss.

6.22 In either case, I think that the energy for change will come in women's seizing the paradox of our existence, drawing on the power of our liminality for ourselves, reading the Bible as tricksters ourselves. In the spirit of reading like a trickster, let me offer a reflection on one of the Bible's most misogynist comments:

> From woman is the beginning of sin
> and because of her all die (Sir 25:24).

What would happen if ironic women were daring enough to embrace rather than reject this statement? If we said, yes, human reality includes evil and death, and woman encompasses them, just as she encompasses goodness and life? Woman does indeed represent *all* of human reality. Could we then say, truly, that "womankind" is the most generic designation possible for the human race?

WORKS CONSULTED

Albertz, Rainer
    1978   *Persönliche Frömmigkeit and offizielle Religion. Religionsinterner Pluralismus in Israel und Babylon.* Stuttgart: Calwerverlag.

Aletti, Jean-Noël
    1976   "Proverbes 8,22-31. Études de structure." *Bib* 57: 25-37.
    1977   "Séduction et Parole en Proverbes I-IX." *VT* 27: 129-44.

Bailey, Lloyd R., Sr.
    1979   *Biblical Perspectives on Death.* Philadelphia: Fortress.

Boström, Gustav
    1935   *Proverbiastudien: die Weisheit und das fremde Weib in Sprüche 1-9.* Lunds Universitäts Arsskrift 30,3. Lund: C. W. K. Gleerup.

Camp, Claudia V.
    1985   *Wisdom and the Feminine in the Book of Proverbs.* Bible and Literature Series, 11. Sheffield, U.K.: JSOT/Almond.

Craven, Toni
    forthcoming   "Women Who Lied for the Faith." In *Justice and the Holy. Essays in Honor of Walter Harrelson.* Ed. Douglas A. Knight and Peter J. Paris. Atlanta: Scholars Press.

Geertz, Clifford
    1975   "Common Sense as a Cultural System." *Antioch Review* 35:5-26.

Gilbert, Maurice
    1979   "Le discours de la Sagesse en Proverbes, 8." Pp. 202-18 in *La sagesse de l'ancien testament.* BETL 51. Leuven: Leuven University Press.

Habel, Norman
    1972   "The Symbolism of Wisdom in Proverbs 1-9." *Int* 26: 131-57.

Humbert, Paul
    1937   "La femme étrangère du Livre des Proverbes." *Revue des Études Sémitiques* 6:40-64.
    1939   "Les adjectifs 'Zâr' et 'Nokri' et la femme étrangère." Pp. 259-66 in *Mélanges Syriens offerts à M. René Dussaud* I. Bibliothèque Archéologique et Historique, 30. Paris: Librairie Orientalisk Paul Geunther.

Johanson, Sheila
    1976   "'Herstory' as History: A New Field or Another Fad?" Pp. 400-30 in *Liberating Women's History.* Ed. Berenice Carroll. Urbana, IL: University of Illinois Press.

Jung, Carl
　1956　"On the Psychology of the Trickster Figure." Trans. R. F. C. Hull. Pp. 195-211 in *The Trickster: A Study in American Indian Mythology.* Ed. Paul Radin. New York: Philosophical Library.

Kerenyi, Karl
　1956　"The Trickster in Relation to Greek Mythology." Trans. R. F. C. Hull. Pp. 173-91 in *The Trickster: A Study in American Indian Mythology..* Ed. Paul Radin. New York: Philosophical Library.

Lang, Bernhard
　1975　*Frau Weisheit.* Düsseldorf: Patmosverlag.

Lévi-Strauss, Claude
　1963　*Structural Anthropology.* Trans. Claire Jacobson and Brooke Grundfest Schoepf. New York: Basic Books.

McKane, William
　1970　*Proverbs: A New Approach.* Philadelphia: Westminster.

Mendenhall, George E.
　1974　"The Shady Side of Wisdom." Pp. 319-34 in *A Light Unto My Path: Old Testament Essays in Honor of Jacob M. Myers.* Gettysburg Theological Studies IV. Ed. Howard N. Bream, Ralph D. Heim and Carey Moore. Philadelphia: Temple University Press.

Meyers, Carol
　1983　"Gender Roles and Genesis 3:16 Revisited." Pp. 337-54 in *The Word of the Lord Shall Go Forth.* Ed. Carol Meyers and M. O'Connor. Winona Lake, IN: Eisenbrauns.

Niditch, Susan
　1979　"The Wronged Woman Righted: An Analysis of Genesis 38." *HTR* 72: 143-49.

Ortner, Sherry B.
　1974　"Is Female to Male as Nature is to Culture?" Pp. 67-88 in *Woman, Culture and Society.* Ed. Michelle Zimbalist Rosaldo and Louise Lamphere. Stanford: Stanford University Press.

Pelton, Robert D.
　1980　*The Trickster in West Africa: A Study of Mythic Irony and Sacred Delight.* Hermeneutics: Studies in the History of Religions. Berkeley: University of California Press.

Radin, Paul
　1956　*The Trickster: A Study in American Indian Mythology.* New York: Philosophical Library.

Savill, Sheila
　1978　*Pears Encyclopedia of Myths and Legends.* Vol. 4: *Oceania and Australia, the Americas.* London: Pelham Brooks.

Scott, R. B. Y.
    1972   "Wise and Foolish, Righteous and Wicked." Pp. 146-65 in *Studies in the Religion of Ancient Israel*. VTSupp 23. Leiden: E. J. Brill.

Snijders, Lambertus A.
    1954   "The Meaning of zar in the Old Testament." *OTS* 10:1-154.

Talmon, Shmarjahu
    1963   "'Wisdom' in the Book of Esther." *VT* 13:419-55.

Thompson, Stith, ed.
    1966   *Tales of the North American Indians*. Bloomington and London: Indiana University Press, 1929. Midland Books.

Trible, Phyllis
    1978   *God and the Rhetoric of Sexuality*. Philadelphia: Fortress.

Turner, Victor
    1977   *The Ritual Process*. Chicago: Aldine Publishing Company, 1969. Cornell Paperbacks.

Whybray, Robert N.
    1968   *The Succession Narrative: A Study of II Sam. 9-20 and I Kings 1 and 2*. Studies in Biblical Theology. Second Series, 9. Naperville, IL: Alec R. Allenson.

Williams, James G.
    1982   *Women Recounted: Narrative Thinking and the God of Israel*. Bible and Literature Series, 6. Sheffield: Almond Press.

Yee, Gale A.
    1980   "An Analysis of Prov. 8:22-31 According to Style and Structure." *ZAW* 94: 48-65.

OUT OF THE SHADOWS
Genesis 38; Judges 4:17-22; Ruth 3

Johanna W. H. Bos
Louisville Presbyterian Theological Seminary

ABSTRACT

This essay attempts to delineate the role of three women as they challenge patriarchy from within patriarchal structures. Tamar challenges the notion that male initiative alone advanced the promises of God to the ancestors of Israel. Yael challenges the patriarchal view of female identity as derived from connections to males, as well as the patriarchal restriction of the public sphere as reserved for males. Ruth makes an unlikely alliance with Naomi, which she serves throughout the narrative, also in ch. 3. This alliance provides a counter-theme especially to the betrothal alliance, and thereby challenges patriarchy. All three women use some form of a ruse to achieve their goal. This may be overt deception, as Tamar's, or subtle deception in leaving a man in his self-deceived state, as Yael's, or, as Ruth's, the ruse of catching a man by surprise in the dark.

0.1 Three women. Each one goes to meet a man outside. Three women reason with the foxes. Each woman is successful in what she sets out to achieve. They outwit their masters and accomplish survival. Three tricks and events change their course.

0.2 The title for this essay is taken from an observation made by Patricia Meyer Spacks (9), that "feminist critics, by raising new questions, have brought unexpected shapes out of the shadows...." The quest of feminist critics of the Bible has at least validated the claim that women are present in the text in a significant way. Women have their place in the story of faith, they are being brought out of the shadows. The "shape" of these women and their activities are to a certain degree predictable and expected, dependent as the women are on the dominant structures of their society. Yet, as I hope to show, women's activities are also unpredictable and unexpected.

0.3   I approach the biblical text from a feminist perspective, which seeks both to uncover androcentrism in the texts and their interpretations and to make the women in these texts visible as movers of events. In addition, I approach the text from a religious perspective, which I define broadly as the expectation that the text is more than a reflection of socio-cultural realities. The narratives before us also carry a religious bias.

0.4   The thesis of this paper is that within the socio-cultural and religious framework of their society, Tamar, Yael, and Ruth are depicted as making autonomous choices—autonomous in the sense that they are not dependent on someone else's authority. Because of their status as a subordinate group, the women exercise their choices by using stratagems, ruses, or tricks; they act autonomously as members of a weak group, using the strategies available to such people.[1]

0.5   Each woman steps in at a critical juncture in the life of a family or larger group and brings about a positive turn in events, which were moving in a negative direction. By staying a step ahead of the males who have power over them, the women thus advance not only their own well-being but also that of the community.

0.6   Insofar as the community of these women is a patriarchy, the women can be said to advance the well-being of patriarchy. Yet the community is more than the patriarchal group. On a theological level, the well-being of the community is of enormous importance, since its well-being is founded on divine promises. The landscape of the text is dominated by God's choice on behalf of the creation, focussed in God's choice of Israel. The choice of Tamar is not merely for the continuation of the patriarchal family embodied in the house of Judah; it is a choice for the building of a house which reflects God's choice for Israel and for the creation.

1. Method

1.1   As there is a variety of feminist approaches to a text, so there is a number of possible ways to focus analysis of the text. This essay makes use of a broad literary method, which Alter describes as "the manifold varieties of minutely discriminating attention to the artful use of language, to the shifting play of ideas, conventions, tone, sound, imagery,

---

[1] I agree with Naomi Steinberg (4.4) that both men and women are depicted as using such strategies, and that they are basically indicative of roles available to those who lack power to achieve their ends in other ways. Since Israelite women would *ipso facto* belong to such a group, they are more often shown as making use of deception than are men.

syntax, narrative viewpoint, compositional units, and much else" (12). In part, the different emphases in my literary analysis of these stories arise out of the differences among the narratives themselves; in part, I deal with these stories differently for the sake of exploring a range of foci. In each case the results should prove to be relevant to the feminist theological inquiry.

1.2   A common element in the focus will be to view the narratives as examples of a type-scene. According to Alter (51-59), one type-scene in biblical narrative is that of "the encounter with the future betrothed at a well." The ingredients of this scene, roughly described, are: 1. The future bridegroom (or surrogate) goes to a foreign land. 2. He encounters a young woman at a well. 3. Someone draws water. 4. The women run home to tell of the arrival of the stranger. 5. Betrothal takes place.

1.3   I suggest that Genesis 38, Judges 4:17-22, and Ruth offer "counter-type-scenes" to the betrothal type-scene.[2] By "counter" I refer to a reversal which takes place in the turn of events, as well as in the arrangement of the central characters. Like the betrothal type-scene, it looks as if the counter-type-scene is about a male in pursuit of success/fortune. But soon loss of life threatens the male and his group, and events take a downward turn. A woman then moves to the center of the narrative to change the course of events toward success/increase of life.

1.4   The main ingredients of this counter-type-scene are: 1. The "foreign" element is introduced in various ways. The male may indeed travel, or settle somewhere (as in the case of Judah and Elimelek), or he may be in "odd," other, and therefore foreign, circumstances (as Barak and Sisera). 2. There is an encounter of male and female, but it is initiated by the woman. The meeting takes place outside. Instead of the well with its symbolism of fertility, there is a substitution of another symbol (as the threshing floor). 3. The encounter involves deception of some sort. The deception is most clear in Tamar's trick of dressing as someone she is not, so that Judah does not recognize her. Yael's deception consists of leaving Sisera deceived as to her true alliances. Ruth's presence in an unexpected place under cover of darkness is a less obvious and more subtle form of deception. In all three stories the deception theme is spun out in terms of an ironic use of verbs for "seeing," "noticing," "knowing." 4. The encounter results in some type

---

[2] The possibility of a counter-type-scene is suggested by Alter himself in regard to the second chapter of Ruth (58). James Williams makes the same suggestion for the entire story of Ruth (84-88). I agree with his analysis but would want to extend the scheme to other narratives.

of gift. In Genesis and Ruth, the gifts of objects of identification and grain respectively are symbolic for the gift of life to come. In Judges, the gift is demanded from the woman by the man and Yael's gift of liquid/life is the contrasting symbol for the "gift" of death which she will hand Sisera shortly. 5. The women leave the place of the encounter, and success is announced. Success for Tamar and Ruth is related to life and giving birth; for Yael, it is related to Sisera's death. Because Sisera is Israel's enemy, his death implies the gift of life for Israel.

2. A Righteous Woman (Genesis 38)

2.1 From Rabbinic times, the odd placement of Gen 38 has caused problems for biblical exegetes and commentators. At the beginning of the stories about Joseph, just when the plot begins to thicken, this chapter on Judah and his adventures seems a disturbing interruption of the narrative flow. A variety of principles which may have guided the redactors has been proposed in the course of biblical scholarship. Sometimes these principles are sought in key phrases, sometimes in the concern or content of the story. (cf. Alter; Cassuto).

2.2 In the fervent discourse as to placement, the characters in this narrative disappeared into the mist of scholarly research until they were barely seen or heard. By focussing more directly on the text, rather than on the problem of its placement, we may hope to recover the actions of the characters and their significance. For the text analysis I have relied on S. Bar Efrat's suggestions (157).

2.3 Narrative Technique
2.3.1 The story divides into five units:

> Vv. 1-11: Introduction and description (Bar Efrat's "Summary")
> Vv. 12-19: Scene I
> Vv. 20-23: Interlude
> Vv. 24-26: Scene II
> Vv. 27-30: Scene III

2.3.2 The first part of the Introduction (vv. 1-6) places the entire cast of characters on the stage and presents a fast time flow, a feature typical of such a unit. A long span of time, including major movements on the part of a main character, marriage, offspring, and that offspring's marriage are covered in a minimum of words. We note that Judah and Tamar appear at the beginning and the end of the unit respectively, thus surrounding the other characters who will be removed from the stage gradually, either by death or inaction (the exception to this removal is Chirah, who functions as a shadow image to Judah).

2.3.3 In the second part of the Introduction (vv. 7-11), events still move at fair speed, but the introduction of speech (vv. 8 and 11) slows the action. This slowing down is reinforced by the listing of detailed actions with motivation recorded. In v. 9 Onan refuses the possibility of impregnating Tamar because he knows that the resulting offspring would not be his. In v. 11 Judah sends Tamar home under the pretense of a promise, in reality (as the text points out) because he is afraid that his third son will die too. Like the son, the father acts in a shortsighted fashion. In the final interchange between Judah and Tamar, Tamar is little more than a passive figure, moved about by the whims of custom and the fears of her father-in-law. She is briefly in the limelight, but the last words of v. 11 show her as relegated to the role of passive bystander. It sounds as if a story which began with Judah in the center will continue that way.

2.3.4 Indeed, the first sentence of the first scene (vv. 12-19) seems to bear out that Judah and his efforts to ensure his family's continuation will remain in the center. Another character, Judah's wife, disappears from the stage through death, and Judah himself is thereby pushed into the foreground. Abruptly, the focus shifts to Tamar, who, hearing of her father-in-law's movements, goes into action. Vv. 12-14 serve to set the scene: we know who the main actors will be, something of their state of mind, and where the action will take place. The tempo of the story has gradually slowed down, especially in the description of Tamar's movements, which seem almost overburdened with detail. Vv. 15-18 slow the tempo even more, with the repeated statement of Judah's misperception of Tamar's identity and the intricate bargaining for a pledge. In this last section Tamar receives a voice, one which she will continue to use at appropriate times. The last part of the unit, vv. 18b-19, shows a speeding up of the tempo and provides a partial resolution of tension, for the listener is told that Tamar's ploy has been successful, that she had conceived. In a few words the activities are concluded satisfactorily and we find Tamar back in her widow's outfit.

2.3.5 The interlude (vv. 20-23), with its humorous overtones, serves to relax the tension. These verses focus on Judah, who, with his friend Chirah, engages in bewildered action and conversation. We can sit back and laugh a little at them.

2.3.6 Scene II (vv. 24-26) brings the events tersely to their climax. Again, Judah appears in the first verses as a major character, making major decisions. V. 25 has Tamar as its subject, first acted upon, then going into action. She waits until the last moment to confront Judah, and not until her last words does the damning evidence appear. Judah then speaks for the last time, retracting his sentence by his statement of

Tamar's righteousness. The last words said about him have the effect of removing him, too, from the stage.

2.3.7 The final scene (vv. 27-30) is Tamar's in the company of the midwife. She gives birth not to one, but two sons. In contrast to the introduction of the tale where the activity of giving birth was reserved for Judah's wife, here it is the seemingly infertile one who gives birth.

2.4 Structure of the Narrative on a Verbal Level

2.4.1 The first part of the introduction (vv. 1-6) is crowded with words for conception, giving birth, and naming; fertility reigns (תהר, ותקרא, ותלד). These words are offset in the second part (vv. 7-11) by words for death (וימתהו in v. 7 and וימת in v. 10) and waste (שחת in v. 9). Tamar, who has not conceived, offers a stark contrast to Judah's wife. Words for males abound: son (vv. 3,4, and 5), firstborn (vv. 5 and 7), brother (vv. 8 and 9). Tamar is identified twice without a proper name and in relation to a male: brother's wife (vv. 8 and 9).

2.4.2 Judah's activities, after his initial moving and settling, concern the building and continuation of a family (vv. 2 and 6). In the second part of the introduction he speaks in imperatives, first to Onan (v. 8) and then to Tamar (v. 11). Motivation on Onan's part is indicated by the verb "to know" (v. 9). Judah's motivation is recorded with a כי-clause: "for he thought that this one might die also" (v. 11). A time indicator occurs in the opening sentence but no other time span is mentioned.

2.4.3 Scene I (vv. 12-19) is introduced by an indication of elapsed time which is general, "as time went by." The verb מות occurs again. As in the introduction to the story, Judah is in movement ("he went down" of v. 1 contrasts with "he went up" of v. 12). The specificity of the place and the activity mentioned, the sheepshearing at Timnah, have the effect of slowing the tempo of the story.

2.4.4 V. 13 unexpectedly shifts the focus to Tamar, first as the recipient of a report and then as the one in charge of her own movement (v. 14). Her actions are elucidated by a motivational כי-clause: "for she had noticed. . . ." (ראתה) She then stations herself at the פתח עינים, usually translated as the Enayim entrance/gate, words which literally refer to the "opening of the eyes."[3] The root ראה is used again immediately, this time of Judah who has appeared on the scene, v. 15. Judah, who sees Tamar, is deceived as to her identity. The reason is given in a כי-clause:

---

[3] I owe this insight in first instance to Fokkelien van Dijk Hemmes (Bal et al.: 54).

"for she had covered her face" (v. 15). V. 15 contains the same verb as v. 1: "he drew aside. . . ." The content of his speech (in the polite form, "please, let me," instead of his customary imperative) is justified by another כי-clause: "for he did not know. . . ."

2.4.5   Then, for the first time, Tamar speaks. In her role she asks the one question that matters: "What will you give me?" The dialogue which follows is filled with references to "giving," in contrast to the "taking" which Judah did in the introduction. The last part of v. 18 and all of v. 19 echo parts of the introduction as well: "he went in to her," originally used of Judah and his wife, and "she conceived," consistently applied to Judah's wife in the introduction (vv. 3,4, and 5) are here applied to Tamar.

2.4.6   In the interlude (vv. 20-23) the words "to send" and "to find" are used effectively to create the impression of the fruitless searching engaged in by Judah. The section opens with the phrase "Judah sent" (v. 20) and closes with Judah announcing "I sent" (v. 23). With one exception, all the verses in this unit contain the root מצא (vv. 20,22,23). The words sound almost like a refrain: "he could not find her . . . I could not find her . . . you could not find her." We note the use of קדשה for זונה in the previous section (vv. 15,21,22).

2.4.7   In contrast to the previous units, the climactic Scene II (vv. 24-26) opens with a precise time indicator. "After three months" has the effect of sharply focusing the listener's attention. The phrase "the report came to Judah" (v. 24) parallels the phrase used when Tamar received a report (v. 13). As was the case there, so here also, the report has immediate results. In two verbs Tamar's sentence is pronounced, "Bring her out, she shall be burned." Judah speaks in imperatives again, and Tamar is reduced to her former state of passivity. In v. 25 the verbal form underscores her passivity, "as she was being brought out. . . ." She is now not only suspected of bringing disaster, she has behaved as a זונה. (Note the return to this word. In v. 24 it is used twice in one sentence.) As she is "being brought out," appearing at her most vulnerable, Tamar "sends," a sending which, in contrast to Judah's fruitless sending, is successful. Twice the root נכר occurs. Tamar bids Judah to "look well," and Judah "takes a close look." This time Judah's looking is a true seeing, as evidenced by his pronouncement of Tamar's righteousness. "She is more righteous than I," Judah declares and once more a crucial כי-clause follows: "because I did not give her to Shelah my son" (a clause which picks up on the key verb "to give" from the scene on the road). The unit ends with the verb ידע, in the sense of sexual intimacy; the use of the root will be commented on below.

2.4.8   The last scene (vv. 27-30) provides a precise time indicator as did the previous one: "At the time of her giving birth. . . ." The details of the birth process draw attention to the giving of life in which Tamar is involved against all expectation.

2.5   *The Level of the Narrative World*

2.5.1   On this level we consider the development of characters and events. Judah, who receives a great deal of attention in the first eleven verses, heads the cast of characters. He is in charge in the introduction, the sun around which the satellites of family and friends move. He sees, he takes, he impregnates. His wife, in proper response, conceives, gives birth, and names. All is well in this family, and what Judah set out to do, establishing and continuing a family, is headed for success. With an eye on the future, Judah "takes" once more, a wife for his oldest son: Tamar.

2.5.2   When things begin to decline, with first Er, then Onan dead, Judah holds the reins of the household still firmly in his hands. He orders Tamar to live at her father's house. Judah holds Tamar responsible or at least is suspicious of her responsibility for the deaths of his sons. When he sends her home, he thinks to act in the best interest of his family and of himself, if not in that of Tamar. The audience has at this point a different view from Judah, since it has been informed of the cause of the two deaths and knows that they are not attributable to Tamar. Tamar is told that Shelah will be her next husband and goes to her father's house. The audience is not informed as to her thoughts about Judah's promise. By ascribing motivation to both Onan and Judah, the narrator introduces a factor of shortsighted self-interest into the story. Onan "wastes" because he does not want to "give." Judah sends Tamar home because he does not want his youngest son to die also. He therefore attempts to sever relations with Tamar. Understandable though Judah's concern may be, he too is acting out of self-interest, rather than on the basis of his responsibility towards Tamar. Ironically, his self-interest will be served not by severing his relations with her but by the closest connection with her.

2.5.3   Tamar, unlike Judah's wife, has not responded in the way a wife should, by conceiving, giving birth, and naming. She seems to be, moreover, a threat to the life of the male family members. Again, the audience knows that, at least in one of the two sexual relations, Tamar has not been the cause of not producing life. Yet she does not protest. In contrast to Judah and his wife, Tamar appears shadow-like, unsubstantial, and surrounded by death. Her silence and obedience in returning to her former home finalize her passivity and uselessness to the community.

2.5.4 By revealing certain information, the story creates an expectant tension. We know that God, and not Tamar, is responsible for the deaths of two of Judah's children. We know that at least two of the male characters are not behaving as they ought to and fail specifically in responsibility toward Tamar. We do not know what Tamar makes of it all. Enough unease has been created to leave the audience in doubt as to what will happen next.

2.5.5 The initial verses of Scene I focus attention on Judah. Focus then shifts abruptly to Tamar. When the audience is told that she heard about Judah's planned outing, it receives the first inkling that Tamar's passivity may not have been total. She has kept herself informed about the doings of her father-in-law. Literally the text reads: "It was told to Tamar." The ones who do the telling are not named. They move between the protagonists, providing vital pieces of information or withholding them. They are more shadowy than Tamar, yet their report causes immediate movement, here on the part of Tamar, later on the part of Judah. The phrasing of the report is telling. It opens with the word הנה, a word which serves to draw attention: "Look at what is happening here!" Judah is called not by his own name but "your father-in-law," emphasizing his relation to Tamar, for whom he has responsibility—responsibility he has not yet fulfilled.

2.5.6 The stage is thus set for Tamar to act. The tempo of the story slows down, providing a view of Tamar in detail. The piling up of verbs in v. 24 highlights the contrast with her former passive state. The same verb used for her retirement to her father's house is used here for her stationing herself at the roadside. This new stationing marks the turning point of Tamar's role in the story and indicates an active waiting instead of an obedient response to the male who rules over her. Tamar sits at the "eye opener" by her own choice; she is not sent here as she had been sent home by Judah. So she sits and waits, wrapped in clothes that give a clear sexual signal; she, who had been dependent on the approaches of the men around her in regard to her sexual life, takes matters into her own hands. She does this because she has noticed that Judah's youngest son is grown and she "had not been given to him as a wife."

2.5.7 Judah enters, and the first report about him is that he "notices." Unlike Tamar's noticing, however, which is true seeing, his noticing deceives him. Twice the text states his blindness: "he thought her to be a whore . . . he did not know that she was his daughter-in-law" (vv. 15 and 16). It is possible, as many commentators think, that this emphasized ignorance provides Judah with an excuse for his subsequent actions. More importantly, these two phrases draw attention to the flaw in Judah's character which was first hinted at in v. 11. His behavior toward Tamar shows lack of righteousness, and so he involves himself in deeds of which he cannot see the true impact. Once he "drew aside" to establish a family, and death threatened to overcome this family. This threat he sought to circumvent. At this moment he "draws aside" to lie with a prostitute and does not know that in so doing he is involved in establishing a family. He thinks to have temporary pleasure and is willing to give something in return. What in truth he is giving, he has no notion about.

2.5.8 Tamar responds in a way appropriate to her role. She speaks here for the first time and it is noteworthy that her first words concern a gift. A gift had been withheld from her, one which was her due. She now demands a gift, and does not proceed with matters at hand on trust but asks for a pledge. Alter (9) has compared the seal, cord, and staff to a person's major credit cards. We should probably think also in terms of driver's license and passport, since it is Judah's identity which is involved. Later, when faced with the returned pledge, Judah recognizes himself.

2.5.9 Judah gives what is demanded: "he gave . . . he entered . . ." (v. 18). Tamar achieves what she set out to get: "she conceived by him." The audience, at least, is assured of the successful outcome of Tamar's ruse. As in the introduction, the listener knows more than the characters, since Tamar herself can hardly have known already about her success. She retires in a quick sequence of verbs into her old skin: "She arose, left, put aside, dressed . . ." (v. 19). The last word of the scene is "widow." It may look as if she is "back home" in her former state of passivity. But this time the narrator has put a little more in the balance for Tamar. In reality she possesses Judah's gifts. Not only does she have the pledge, she has the gift of life. But life is not a sure thing, not yet.

2.5.10 The relatively lengthy description of Judah's attempt to send the woman what he promised delineates his character more clearly and at the same time provides comic relief. Not a man to renege on his promises (!), and desirous as well to reclaim his property, Judah sends the promised kid. He delegates the task, however, to his friend Chirah. Perhaps he would rather not be seen asking around for a whore, however politely rephrased into a "cult prostitute" she may be. The local people have indeed not seen a *qedeshah* and so they speak the truth. The passage echoes: "not here . . . could not find her . . . find her . . . find her!" The paterfamilias, sure of his place in the world, is not willing to sacrifice his dignity for a whore. "Let her keep . . . lest we become ridiculous" (generously including his friend in his face-saving efforts, v. 23). Judah, not wishing to be exposed, will shortly be exposed by one whose existence he has almost forgotten.

2.5.11 After the humorous interlude the audience is brought to attention with the precise time indicator of Scene II: "After three months . . . ." Tamar is identified by her proper name as well as by her relationship to Judah. Her shame casts shame on Judah, by virtue of their relationship. Judah is in full command of the situation; his own follies are safely behind him, hidden from public view. Tamar's folly cannot be hidden and she must be punished for it. He opens his mouth for two commands and Tamar's passive, useless existence is about to come to an end. The punishment is unusually harsh, but it is Judah's right to decree the kind of sentence she must receive.

2.5.12 At the point when she appears most vulnerable, Tamar acts for the last time. She sends a message to her father-in-law. Judah is named by this relational term alone for the second time in the story (the first occurred in v. 13). Both times occur at a point where Tamar is about to make a decisive move. Whereas he should have acted on her behalf, Judah's actions toward Tamar have been negative and deceptive and finally destructive. Tamar's matter-of-fact message consists of a brief description and a request: "By the man . . . I am pregnant . . . look well . . . whose . . ." (v. 25).

2.5.13 Judah takes a close look and finally sees. Faced with himself, he is able to see both himself and Tamar. He sees that what he should have given he did not give and that what he gave set the trap to show his own unrighteousness. "She is more righteous than I," Judah declares, "because I did not give. . . ." High praise for one whom he once sent home as a jinxed barren wife. The use of the root ידע for sexual intimacy in v. 26, and for the first time in a story rich in descriptions of sexual activity, is striking. Judah did not know Tamar; now that he knows her, the need for further knowledge is over.

2.5.14 Scene III concludes events on a triumphant note. Two lives are produced to balance the loss of the two sons of Judah recorded in the introduction. Judah and those around him have disappeared, leaving Tamar in the center of the stage, supported by the midwife. A story that began about a male's movements ends by recording the giving of life on the part of the one who seemed incapable of it. Twice the word הנה points the listener to the birth process. Death and threat of death have been overcome by life.

2.6 Structure of the Narrative on a Thematic Level

2.6.1 The major themes of the patriarchal and matriarchal cycles in Genesis are related to God's promises of progeny and land. The promises are often depicted as impossible, unlikely, or endangered, and unlikely characters play a vital part in the continuation of family against the odds. Gen 38 fits well within these concerns. The motif of barrenness is frequently used to emphasize the fragility of the promises. There are other threats, such as family strife, or fights with the inhabitants of the land. All complexity of human nature is brought to bear on the intricate development of the future.

2.6.2 Besides threats and dangers, there are signs of ongoing life, of prosperity, and of fertility. The majority of the Genesis stories can be placed somewhere between these two poles of threat and hope. The betrothal type-scene should be placed at the positive end, whereas the counter-type-scene, as we meet it in Gen 38, swings from positive to negative and back. Success/life is snatched from the jaws of failure/death. The threat to life is, for the most part, due to an explicit failure of the male characters. It is due to a woman's actions and her risk-taking that life ensues.

2.6.3 Where is the androcentrism of this text located? An obvious bias is found in the lack of open condemnation of Judah, who behaved irresponsibly and destructively toward Tamar. The outcome of the story may seem equally androcentric, in placing Tamar on the throne of motherhood, giving birth to two male children, her very place a safeguard for the patriarchal structures (See Fuchs 1985a: 128-29).

2.6.4 Androcentric bias is also clearly visible in the interpretations of the story which show difficulty in dealing with a woman as a central character. Indeed, many questions are raised by this story for the interested observer—levirate marriage, sacred prostitution, the law of primogeniture, all are operative factors in the narrative. But among these matters of interest, the most astounding fact frequently manages to get lost; i.e., that in this story a woman's view of reality, of the characters around her, of herself, and of her own possibilities wins out, that her actions based on this view prevail and change the direction of events.

2.6.5 The story of Tamar points in the direction of a gynocentric bias. The men in the story are wrongheaded irresponsible bunglers, who don't see straight. They are shown up as such by Tamar, who notices correctly and who causes Judah such an "eye-opener" that his view of reality is restored. The tone in which the men are discussed, summarily dispatched by God, or acting as if they were in charge and all the while making fools of themselves, points to a gynocentric bias as well.

2.6.6 If there were indeed women story-tellers in ancient Israel, as Campbell (22) has suggested, such a circle might be the most natural matrix for the story of Tamar. Although Cassuto and Alter have shown a strong connection between the story of Tamar and the Joseph cycle which surrounds it, there are others who maintain that the story does not belong here. In the end we may have to admit that in some ways the story fits and in some ways it does not. The verbal links between Gen 38 and the Joseph cycle are undeniable, but after all is said and done, the story remains a bit of a maverick in its surroundings. In the Joseph cycle the emphasis is overwhelmingly male, more so than in the preceding material. Apart from the negative portrayal of Potifar's wife, women do not play a role in the Joseph stories. Gen 38 not only describes a woman as a central character but it also contains a rather unsavory episode from a patriarchal point of view. Not only are the sexual exploits of father Judah unorthodox compared to the other patriarchs, but in this tale God cares so little for the patriarchal offspring that two of the sons are dispatched by the divine hand. Tone and content reflect the perspective of a dominated group, which for the sake of survival mocks the oppressor and gets the better of him. Gen 38 allows one to smile at the solemn face of patriarchy.

2.6.7 In the context of the Joseph cycle, on the other hand, the Tamar-Judah story provides a contrast to the Joseph-Potifar's wife story. It also presents an apt character portrayal of Judah on the basis of what has gone before, as well as a preparation for the way he will appear in the sequel. The outcome of the story, moreover, establishes the line of David. Not a tale to dismiss lightly.

2.6.8 Both patriarchy and counter-voice can be heard in the narrative of Tamar and her family. Tamar does not change the patriarchal structures of her world, but her story challenges at least the notion, which may be a byproduct of such structures, that the promises of God are advanced through male initiative alone.

3. *A Blow For Freedom (Judges 4:17-22)*
3.1 Judg 4:17-22 is an unusual text in a number of ways. This brief story about a Kenite woman named Yael is a part of a story about another woman, Deborah. The roles of both women are unusual. Deborah is a warrior/leader, although she appoints a man, Baraq, to do the actual fighting. This man's task is taken over in part by the woman Yael, who kills the general of the Canaanite army. Finally, the story of

Yael is preserved in two versions, Judg 4:17-22 and Judg 5:25-26. The discussion which follows focuses on the first account.

3.2   Judg 4:17-22

(17) Sisera fled on foot
to the tent of Yael,
wife of Hever, the Kenite,
for there was peace
between Yavin, king of Hazor,
and the house of Hever, the Kenite.
(18) Then came out Yael
to meet Sisera.
She said to him:
"Turn now, my lord,
turn now to me.
Have no fear!"
He turned to her,
to her tent,
and she closed it with a curtain.
(19) He said to her:
"Please, some water to drink,
for I am thirsty."
She opened a milk jug,
gave him to drink and closed it.
(20) He said to her:
"Stand at the tent opening.
If a man comes,
and asks you and says:
'Is there a man here?'
say: 'No!'"
(21) Then took Yael,
wife of Hever,
the tent peg and picked up
the hammer in her hand.
She came to him quietly,
she drove the peg in his head
and it hit the ground;
he, stunned, passed out and died.
(22) Then, look, Baraq in pursuit of Sisera.
Then came out Yael
to meet him.
She said to him:
"Come, and I'll show you
the man you are after."
So he came to her;
and, look, Sisera
fallen dead—
the peg in his head.

3.2.1. Obscurities in Hebrew occur in v. 18 where שמיכה is a hapax: in v. 21 where the words רקה and צנח are not clear, and where the order of the verbs of the last phrase is awkward. What, or whom, does Yael cover? Where does she hit Sisera and in what position is he when she hits him?

3.2.2 שמיכה (v. 18) has received a number of different readings and interpretations. In spite of the lack of certainty, there is general agreement that a type of covering is indicated, as also appears from the versions and translations. There is also agreement that Sisera is the object and that Yael covers him with something. This covering action is mentioned twice, once in v. 18 and again in v. 19. What precisely she covers him with is left to the imagination. Word-plays on "open" and "close/cover" indicate the hidden intent of Yael. Most commentators view Yael's covering of Sisera as creating a false sense of trust once she has lured him into her tent.

3.2.3 It seems possible to view her actions as both more natural and less deceptive by assuming the object of כסה in the first case to be the tent or its opening, and in the second case the container with milk. The most natural action on Yael's part would be to close the tent opening once Sisera is inside and the milk-container once she has opened it. The action of covering Sisera, once he is inside her tent, is less easily explained and has occasioned numerous speculations. The word play remains in force whether Sisera or a lifeless object is understood. While Yael is busy opening and covering, she is in truth covering her intent towards Sisera.

3.2.4 In v. 21 רקה (literally "the thin place") has received a variety of translations from "skull" to "brains" to "temple." I take it to stand *pars pro toto* for "head." צנח occurs only three times in the Hebrew Bible and is elsewhere translated "to come down" (Josh 15:18=Jud 1:41; but see NEB). Nicholson (265) suggests that the common element between the three texts is the downward movement. I take רקה as the subject of ותצנח; i.e., Sisera's head came down on the ground after Yael hammered the peg into it. This suggestion relieves the problem of having to imagine that the peg went in on one side of Sisera's head, came out on the other, and went subsequently into the ground.

3.2.5 For the phrase והוא נרדם ויעף וימת in v. 21 RSV reads, "as he was lying fast asleep from weariness. So he died." With some variations, this reading is a common translation of the phrase, and it assumes that Yael killed her adversary in his sleep. The awkwardness of the verb order is that it makes sleep follow being hit with the tent peg, and faintness follow sleep, instead of the other way around. The odd sequence has occasioned much comment; Lagrange, for example, suggests a translation based on the Hebrew ויצנח בין ברכיה ויעף וימת, "he twitched convulsively between her knees, fell lifeless to the ground and died" (74). The text can be read as it stands by taking the root רדם to mean "stunned" (cf. Ps. 76:7), and יעף "to be weary/lack strength," in the sense of "to pass out." Sisera is stunned, collapses, and dies. The sequence of verbs with similar meaning creates a slow-motion effect similar to the one operative in Judg 5.[4]

3.2.6   The notion that Sisera was not lying down when Yael struck him is supported by the use of the root נפל in both accounts (Judg 4:22 and Judg 5:27). This verb is always used of someone who is fallen from a once upright position. I conclude that Sisera was probably sitting down, that Yael hit his head from behind, striking by luck or skill on the most vulnerable spot.

3.2.7   As Yael's deceptiveness has been exaggerated, so both her victim's helplessness and her violence receive an emphasis in the translations and commentaries which the text does not warrant. The violence of the story is disturbing, but so is all the violence which one encounters in the Bible, whether it is perpetrated by women or by men.

3.2.8   Although the phrase חבר הקני does not present a textual problem, a comment on its meaning and implications is warranted. Soggin suggests the translation "Kenite group" for these two words. Yael then becomes "the woman of the Kenite group" in v. 17. (Soggin: 1981b, 74-75). The mention of חבר הקני in Judg 4:11 would point to the fact that a clan of the Kenites had separated from the main group in the Negeb and settled near Kedesh. This suggestion is attractive on logical grounds, since it makes Sisera's flight in the direction of the Kenite tents more understandable. There can be no objection to it on linguistic grounds, since חבר means "group." Moreover, this interpretation would highlight the courage and independence of Yael's choice, since she makes it over against her clan, not just her immediate family. There remains as an objection the uniform tradition of translating this Hebrew noun with the proper name Hever. In addition, an awkwardness results in v. 21 where הקני is missing following חבר, and a definite article would be expected before חבר if a noun were intended. A more plausible suggestion than Soggin's is that of Malamat, who considers Hever to be a personification of a nomadic subdivision (145). While I retain the

---

[4] Cf. Alan Hauser's observation about Judg 5:25-26 that "the use of so many words for the two acts of offering the milk and seizing the weapon gives a 'slow motion' effect to Jael's deeds . . ." (36).

traditional translation in this case, I agree with Malamat that a group of families is indicated by the name Hever. Yael therefore makes her decision in opposition to her clan.

3.3 Judg 4:17-22 is more episodic than Gen 38. My analysis deals with the following questions: 1. Who speaks? What does the speaker say? How is it said? 2. Who acts and of what do the actions consist? 3. Who looks where does the person look, what do they see? (Bal *et al.*, 10-11 and 21).

3.4 Who Speaks?
3.4.1 Of the three characters in the account, only two speak. One of them, Sisera, needs no introduction since he appears in the preceding verses as the general of the Canaanite army, which has just been defeated by Baraq. In fact, Sisera's flight on foot has been recorded already (v. 15). Sisera is named in Judg 4:17-22 four times, each time without closer identification.

3.4.2 Yael's name occurs four times as well. When she is introduced, she is identified by her tribe, and the tribe's alliance. Four names besides Yael's occur: Hever, Yavin, Kenite, and Hazor. Hever, with the tribal identification, is immediately repeated (v. 17). Yael's identity is derived; her name is covered by the names of the men to whom she is connected. Without tribal identification Hever's name occurs once more, when Yael collects her instruments for the assassination (v. 21). The woman is called Yael (without other identification) on the two occasions when she goes out—once to meet the pursued, Sisera, and once to meet the pursuer, Baraq.

3.4.3 Yael has the first and last words in the story. Both times she addresses a man outside (ותצא יעל לקראת סיסרה, v. 18 // ותצא יעל לקראתו, v. 22). Both times she invites a man into her tent, but her words in v. 18 leave all to the assumption of Sisera, whereas in v. 22 Yael provides an explicit reason for Baraq to come in. Each time Yael's words meet with a positive response. Sisera turns her way, into the tent, Baraq comes to see what she has to show him. The invitation to Sisera is pressing, but polite and persuasive: "Turn now, my lord, turn now to me." The words, "have no fear," strike an ironic note. The woman tells the warrior not to be afraid! On one level Yael's words carry the reassurance the man needs that she belongs to a group at peace with Sisera's master. On another level, the word "fear" strikes a discordant note on what should be an occasion which contains no threat, since it is based on the assumption of *shalom*. Yael's last words in the story, addressed to Baraq, do not require politeness or persuasion. She has done her deed; all that remains is to show what she has done.

3.4.4 Like Yael's, Sisera's speech undergoes change. His tone to Yael is polite when he asks for a drink, "please, some water to drink," and becomes short and demanding when his request has been fulfilled. Sisera has two concerns, of which the most important one, his safety, is mentioned second. He is thirsty and asks first that this immediate need be met. His request for water is put in as few words as possible, indicating perhaps the exhausted state of a man who has been on the run. His second request is more elaborate and has the tone of a general who tells his subordinate precisely what position to take and what to do: "Stand . . . and say." He takes no risks; Yael is not to tell anyone that Sisera is hidden in her tent. Ironically, this seeming return to being the warrior in charge, who issues commands, precedes Sisera's imminent demise.

3.4.5 Sisera's second speech anticipates subtly Baraq's pursuit: "If a man comes . . . is there a man here?" A man will indeed come and view a man, but he will not have to ask; Yael will show Baraq the man he seeks. In a way, Sisera's instructions that Yael deny the presence of a man in her tent also anticipate his death. The man who, even as a fugitive, spoke as one in charge is, in reality, a dead man, "not there"; the woman who was introduced with a derived identity is in the end shown as the one in charge: "Come, I will show you. . . ."

3.5 Who Acts?

3.5.1 In the introduction Sisera is active, even though his activity is the negative one of fleeing. Soon Sisera moves to passivity, even while he issues commands. In the concluding v. 22, Sisera has become entirely passive, providing a spectacle for Baraq; he is "fallen, dead." The two verbs form a contrasting parallel to "fled on foot" of v. 17. In the sequence of verbs of which Sisera is the subject, the only activity not directly connected with death, after he turns toward Yael, is that of speech.

3.5.2 After her elaborate identification, Yael becomes the subject of a verb and stays active throughout. Her coming out to meet Sisera in v. 18 and her words and actions through v. 20 are set against the background of her family or clan alliance. She speaks and acts as the wife/servant. She hides Sisera in her tent; she gives him the liquid which she has at hand and makes a move to stand at the tent opening to peek out. The turn in her actions is dramatic. In v. 21 she is called the wife of Hever—a sign of discord between that identification and the activity she engages in. The quick sequence of verbs in the verses which open, "Then took Yael . . .," show a climactic development: "She picked up . . . came . . . and drove!" The innocuous act of picking up tent peg and hammer, the tenting woman's tools, escalates into the violence of "she drove." The tools are hers; the actions are a startling reversal of the expectations of a female with her family alliances.

3.5.3 Effective with her hammer and peg, Yael kills the general. She then goes out again, this time identified solely as Yael. She goes out to Baraq to show him her success, which we must presume she achieved on the basis of her own choice of allies. Her alliance, against expectation, is to Israel and Israel's God. Sisera's expectation that she would act on her clan's alliance, alluded to by the threefold repetition of Hever, rests on self-deception. Yael's deception consists in counting on Sisera's self-deception. When she goes out to Baraq, she has nothing to hide, "Come, I will show you. . . ."

3.5.4 Yael's action has deprived one man of life and the other of success. Baraq's action is minimal, consisting of pursuit and of viewing the body of the enemy who lies dead at the hand of a woman.

3.5.5 The actions of the characters in the story are for a great part what one would expect. There, the defeated warrior on the run, and here, the victorious one in hot pursuit. Nothing they do is out of character. The fleeing warrior counts on the alliances of the woman he meets, and on her service, to get him out of his precarious circumstances. At first, the woman responds to his requests and acts on his behalf, doing nothing to upset expectations.

3.5.6 Only Yael eventually acts out of character, and she has to depend on Sisera's misperceptions for her plan to work. She therefore reinforces these misperceptions. Sisera shows his trust in her by demanding that she keep watch. Yael's next actions (v. 21) yet hide her intention, for the peg and hammer belonged to a woman's hand. The addition of חבר to Yael's name strengthens the impression that nothing is out of order. The next words might alert the suspicious listener, but not necessarily, since there may have been ordinary reasons for Yael to come up to Sisera quietly. Not until the word רקה appears is Yael's true intent revealed. The tent peg and the hammer in Yael's hand have become tools of destruction. The two instruments together, of course, make the resulting death a sure thing, once she hits the right spot. The woman whose domain is the tent, who sets it up and organizes it, acts here within her domain, but outside of her tasks. Yael's venture into the domain of battle while yet inside her tent is more dramatic than the venture of Deborah.

3.5.7 More than that of Tamar, the story of Yael shows a cracking of the patriarchal structures themselves. To be sure, Yael serves patriarchal

Israel, but her actions break the rules of patriarchy. They are not based on derived identity, on her connection with men, nor on the restrictions of certain activities as belonging to one gender, with the public sphere and its activities reserved for the male. Yael draws the public domain into her tent and acts on her own.

3.6 Who Sees?
3.6.1 Yael's action is told with approval since her choice was on behalf of Israel. This perspective is most clearly present in Judg 5 (see below, par. 3.6.7). Commentators generally view Yael's actions with varying degrees of condemnation. She is said to have violated customs of hospitality while pretending to keep them, thus to have gone overboard in her deception of "poor" Sisera whom she killed while he was fast asleep. Such negative judgments arise most likely because of unspoken assumptions about proper feminine behavior and acceptable codes of social intercourse.

3.6.2 The account shows events from different points of view. The audience sees Sisera running for his life, to a tent. The phrasing implies that he sees "the wife of Hever the Kenite whose house is at peace with Yavin the king of Hazor." Sisera seems to be fleeing toward safe shelter. At the very least, Sisera sees someone who can aid him, with supplies at hand, who can serve as a lookout. He sees falsely, for he is looking in the direction of her clan and not of Yael herself. Even if he saw the tent peg and the hammer in her hand, it would not strike him as out of place. She is Yael-the-wife-of-Hever with her woman's tools. He, Sisera, tells her what to do, where to stand, and what to say.

3.6.3 The audience is allowed to "see" a bit more than Sisera, but only by allusion. Yael comes out as her own person, named by her proper name only. She comes out with a purpose, "to meet Sisera." Sisera, according to 4:3, was a general who had "nine hundred chariots of iron, and oppressed the people of Israel cruelly for twenty years." This kind of man, even when on the run, is not a person one would readily choose to meet. Sisera has come down from his chariot but is surely not unarmed. He remains a trained warrior, no match for an untrained man, let alone an untrained woman. Sisera's fear is naturally not of Yael but of other men: "If a man comes. . . ." That his life may not be safe with her is probably farthest from his thoughts.

3.6.4 What else may Yael have seen in Sisera besides the warrior/oppressor? Judg 5:28-30 provides a clue. Its perspective is that of the women in Sisera's family, who speculate on his delay from the battlefield and surmise that the amassing of booty is the cause. Booty in war has always included rape, and v. 30, "A maiden, two maidens, for each warrior . . . " spells this out. It is a warrior/rapist whom Yael invites to "turn" to her, to whom she offers refreshment; it is the spoiler of women whom she spoils.

3.6.5 We noted earlier Yael's invitation to Sisera to "have no fear" and its introduction of a discordant note. When the scene shifts to inside the tent, the words for "open" and "close" indicate that more is going on than appears on the surface. Amidst the opening and closing, Yael's true intent toward Sisera remains hidden. In v. 21, on the other hand, the motions of both Yael and Sisera come into sharp focus. One sees Yael picking up the tent peg and hammer, driving in the peg in one motion, and Sisera slumping on the ground and dying.

3.6.6 Abruptly, the scene switches to the outside, where Baraq comes into view, seeking the life of the defeated Sisera (v. 22). This scene is introduced by the word הנה, which twice in this verse draws attention to the matter at hand.[5] At that very moment, who would turn up but Baraq! Yael has one last action to perform. She needs to show Baraq, literally to "cause him to see." The audience sees the next scene through Baraq's eyes: "Look (הנה), Sisera fallen dead, the peg in his head!" Deborah's words have come true. No words from Baraq are recorded; one sees him staring wordlessly inside the tent at the glory which is snatched from his grasp.

3.6.7 The perspective of Judg 5 is one-sided in its praise of Yael, viewing her violent deed as a positive one and the fall of Sisera as a death deserved by those who oppose Yhwh (v. 31). Hauser (35) has noted the emphasis of Yael's womanhood, a point made by the poet "to mock the defeated Canaanites." One might equally understand the emphatic praise of the woman Yael to stand in contrast to the cowardice of the men of the previous verse (v. 23). On the other hand Yael's deed is contrasted with the posture of the women in Sisera's household, who wait at home and view the warrior/rapist's actions without criticism.

3.6.8 An androcentric bias does not seem operative in either Judg 4:17-22 or Judg 5:24-27. In Judg 4 two men are rendered powerless. The sense that these men are fools as compared to the women in the story is not present as it was in the Tamar story. Although Sisera is Yael's dupe, he exudes strength even in defeat, and Baraq remains a victorious general. Also, Deborah's words (Judg 4:9) have prepared the way for this event, which is unexpected only in the details.

---

[5] For a discussion of the term הנה as it relates to point of view, see Berlin: 62-63.

3.6.9 Yael, weak by virtue of her womanhood, exercises physical and emotional strength. The ruse does not make her strength less impressive. The reversal of roles in Judg 4 is one in which the powerful (males) show weakness and the weak (females) show strength. This picture makes an apt paradigm for weak Israel, which in the Book of Judges time and again defeats a more powerful enemy. The victories are attributed to God, of course, but there are those who come to the help of God (Judg 5:23). The extraordinary feature of Judg 4 and 5 is that women become the "helpers" through whom God accomplishes victory and that one of them is not a member of the Israelite tribes.

4. A Valiant Woman (Ruth 3:6)[6]

4.1. Of the three women under consideration here, Ruth may well be the most unorthodox in her alliances. Whereas Yael makes a radical break with her natural alliances, Ruth allies herself to a most unlikely partner. The entire story and its development must be viewed in terms of Ruth's statement to Naomi in 1:16-17. The motivational force of Ruth's words and actions is confirmed by Naomi's neighbors to be love. When Ruth has given birth to her son, the women of Naomi's community tell her: ". . . your daughter-in-law who loves you has borne him . . ." (4:15). This pronouncement makes Ruth the subject of the single occurrence of the verb "to love" in the book, with Naomi as the direct object. The most radical reversal of the character arrangement of a betrothal type-scene has taken place: the encounter which occasions the rest of the story is between two women. The outcome too is subtly reversed. Even though a marriage takes place, it becomes the occasion for the one woman to show her love for the other. Moreover, unlike the context of a betrothal, there is ostensibly no advantage for Ruth in her initial alliance to Naomi. The women's circumstances place them in a most vulnerable and weak position. Both are childless and widowed, and both know the experience of foreignness. By joining herself to Naomi, Ruth willingly joins weakness to weakness, death to death.

4.2 Characterization

4.2.1 The characters in Ruth have been established by the time the episode of ch. 3 takes place. Ch. 3 shows character development and change.

---

[6] Much excellent work has been done on the book of Ruth in recent years. This presentation is especially indebted to the work of Phyllis Trible, Edward Campbell, Jr., and D. F. Rauber for insights into the literary structure, major themes, and theological concerns. More recently, Adele Berlin devoted a chapter to Ruth as an example of applied poetic principles to text analysis. This study relies on Berlin's distinction between character and agent in the biblical text as well as on her discussions of point of view and structure.

4.2.2 Throughout the story Naomi is called by her proper name or by a term that relates her to others, "mother-in-law." The verse immediately preceding ch. 3 ends with the word "mother-in-law" (2:23). Ch. 3 begins "Then said to her Naomi, her mother-in-law," the only time that she is identified by both her proper name and her relation to Ruth. At the end of ch. 2, all indications are that Naomi is beginning to wake up to the presence of Ruth and to the responsibility as well as the promise of this presence. In ch. 3 this turn in Naomi's attitude is brought to completion.

4.2.3 Between her elaborate attempt at convincing Ruth to return to Moab (1:8-15) and the concluding scene of ch. 2, when Ruth has come home from gathering grain in the field of Boaz, Naomi's words to Ruth have been few. When Naomi and Ruth reach Bethlehem, Naomi tells the women there, "full did I go, empty the Lord brings me back" (1:21). Ruth's presence does not alleviate Naomi's emptiness. When Ruth offers to gather food for them, Naomi speaks only two words, "Go, my daughter" (2:2). Only at Ruth's return from Boaz' field, does Naomi enter into a more extensive conversation with Ruth. At the beginning of ch. 3, Naomi presents a relatively long speech to Ruth; precisely in this chapter she is called consistently "her mother-in-law." At the end of ch. 3 the role of mother-in-law is completed and Naomi will not be referred to in this way again. At the conclusion of the story (ch. 4), Naomi, once more the empty woman, is called "Naomi, who returned from Moab's fields" (4:3); her emptiness is about to be filled by the birth of her grandchild, after which she is called simply "Naomi" (4:9).

4.2.4 Naomi's counterpart in the story, Boaz, is named in a number of ways in ch. 3. Naomi refers to him as a kinsman of Ruth and herself. From Naomi's perspective Boaz is a candidate for marriage with Ruth. Heretofore Boaz has been identified as an איש גבור חיל and member of Elimelek's family by the narrator (2:1), as "my lord" by Ruth (2:13), and as a "relative" and a "redeemer" by Naomi (2:20). In her speech to Ruth in ch. 3, Naomi calls Boaz a מודעת.

4.2.5 Boaz is called simply "the man" (האיש) four times (3:3,8,16, and 18). This reference parallels the naming "woman" for Ruth. In this part of the story, Ruth and Boaz relate to each other as man and woman. The "man-woman" terminology is one of the ways in which the narrator plays on the ambiguity of the circumstances.[7] It is especially striking

---

[7] E. F. Campbell Jr., has described this as a deliberate play with the ambiguities (131). I believe with Campbell that the narrator's intent is serious rather than merely suggestive and

that Boaz' proper name is absent in the concluding verses, where he is twice referred to, by Ruth and Naomi in turn, as האיש.

4.2.6   Finally, Boaz is named "redeemer" (גאל) by Ruth when she identifies herself to him on the threshing floor. We will return to the significance of this designation.

4.2.7   In this chapter Ruth is not referred to as "the Moabite," an identification added frequently to her name elsewhere in the story (cf. 1:22; 2:2; 4:5, 10). On the threshing floor Ruth calls herself, "Ruth, your servant." Ruth's naming of herself occurs at a crucial point in the story. As Berlin (89) and others have pointed out, the designation "servant" is not self-denigrating. It draws attention to her position vis-à-vis Boaz instead of to her foreignness.

4.2.8   Ruth is called "my daughter" five times in this chapter, three times by Naomi and twice by Boaz. This designation is a standard one from the side of Ruth's elders (cf. 2:1, 8 and 22). In ch. 3 Ruth is also named "woman." Even though Ruth is still addressed as child/daughter, she is becoming more than that, she is also the woman next to the man, Boaz.

4.2.9   Boaz names Ruth with a term of the highest praise אשת חיל. Later, he considers that it should not become public knowledge that "the woman" has come to the threshing floor. In view both of the circumstances and of the sequel, Ruth's identification as "the woman" is telling. Both Ruth's good name and Boaz' name must be protected for all to go well at the city gate. It is not Ruth's foreignness that makes her visit risky but the fact that she is the woman on whose behalf he will act the next day. In the sequel, the word will be picked up when the witnesses at the city gate refer to Ruth as "the woman, who is coming into your house" (4:11).

4.3 Narrative Structure
4.3.1   Following Berlin's model, I find in Ruth 3 these elements: (a) orientation; (b) complicating action and evaluation; (c) resolution.

4.3.2 Orientation (vv. 1-5)
4.3.2.1   This is the only chapter in Ruth which lacks a narrative introduction, opening instead with direct speech. The speech orients the listener to Naomi's point of view and sets up expectations for the events

---

that the listener's speculations as to sexual intercourse on the threshing floor are irrelevant to the story.

to follow. Naomi provides a rationale for her suggestions to Ruth by asking two rhetorical questions. The first makes clear that Naomi is taking responsibility for Ruth's welfare. The second provides a possible solution to the first, since from Naomi's point of view Boaz is the most promising candidate for providing Ruth with a "home." The remainder of Naomi's speech makes her intentions even more clear. Ruth would hardly have to dress in her "Sunday best," and put herself in a compromising situation merely to ask Boaz for advice!

4.3.2.2 With her opening words, Naomi thus registers her intentions, alludes to Boaz' potential, and points to an opportune place for matters to develop. The הנה-clause ("Look, he will be winnowing . . ." v. 2) serves to focus Ruth's attention on the specific place where she may find her potential marriage partner. Moreover, the listeners are now oriented to the place where events will happen. (For the importance of the הנה-clause as representing point of view here, see Berlin: 92).

4.3.2.3 Next, Naomi issues a series of directives to Ruth, which include a reference to the shifting of the initiative to Boaz: "he will tell you what you should do" (v. 4). It looks, then, as if Naomi and Boaz are entirely in charge and Ruth is expected to follow where they lead. Ruth's response to Naomi confirms this expectation, "All that you say I will do" (v. 5). The listeners are oriented neatly to the happenings of the night to come. Yet they know that in the past Ruth has not been one to follow directives from her mother-in-law and that her initiatives have set events in motion. Ruth's words to Naomi thus create a tension and an expectation of their own.

4.3.3 *Complicating Action and Evaluation (vv. 6-15)*
4.3.3.1 Verses 6-7 and 14-15 provide, respectively, the introduction and the conclusion to the scene on the threshing floor. Verses 8-13 report the conversation between Ruth and Boaz. Some reorientation takes place in these sections. Certain expectations are not fulfilled and new expectations and tensions arise.

4.3.3.2 Ruth is the subject of the introductory verses. She "acted according to all that her mother-in-law commanded her" (v. 6). The variation in the phrase occurs in the verb "commanded" for "say" of v. 5. V. 7 introduces some ambiguity. When Boaz has eaten and drunk, the text records: וייטב לבו. This description of Boaz hints at an obstacle to things unfolding exactly according to Naomi's plan (Campbell: 121). Ruth comes "quietly." The difference between Naomi's instructions and what actually happens is small and consists of adding the one word בלט to the verb בוא (cf. Judg 4:21). One may assume on the basis of this word and the sequel, that Ruth deliberately hides from Boaz until he wakes up and notices her. It is not entirely clear whether Naomi's instructions are followed here or whether Ruth introduces a variation in the plot.

4.3.3.3   Vv. 8-13 report the crucial conversation between Ruth and Boaz. When, in the middle of the night, Boaz awakes, he discovers a woman nearby and asks her identity. Ruth answers by giving her proper name with the term "your servant" added. Her answer establishes her as a person in her own right, and at the same time relates her to the man beside her. She makes her request without further encumbrances of politeness, in contrast to her earlier conversation with Boaz (2:10 and 13): "Spread your wings over your servant for you are a redeemer" (v. 9). The word כנף recalls 2:12, where Boaz wished for Ruth recompense from God under whose כנפים she had come to take refuge. On the threshing floor Ruth uses the same image to call Boaz to his task. Nowhere in Ruth is the correspondence between human activity and divine activity so clearly put as in 3:9. Divine recompense must be brought into active operation by Boaz.

4.3.3.4   Subsequently, Ruth provides Boaz with a motivation for acting in her favor, "for you are a redeemer." By appealing to the responsibility of redemption, she calls on a concept that worked powerfully in both the social and the religious sphere in Israel. Redemption laws were intended to function on behalf of those without the capacity to care for themselves. When Naomi received Ruth on her return from her first day in the field, she announced that Boaz was one of their redeemers. That announcement raised high hopes for their future. At the opening of ch. 3 a considerable span of time has passed without a sign that Boaz is going to act on his responsibility. So far, he has been kind and generous but no more than that. With her clever turn of phrase and direct appeal to his duty, Ruth leaves Boaz no option but a direct response. Whereas she does not deceive Boaz in any way, she outwits him certainly. Ruth has not waited until Boaz tells her what to do, but rather she has told him what to do.

4.3.3.5   Boaz responds positively. In his evaluation of Ruth we hear the narrator's evaluation. Like Yael, Ruth is called "blessed." Boaz' assurance that he will do all that Ruth says echoes Ruth's earlier words to Naomi (v. 5) and reverses Naomi's words to Ruth (v. 4). In naming Ruth אשת חיל Boaz places her on a plane parallel to himself, since he was introduced with the words איש גבור חיל in 2:1.

4.3.3.6   Boaz' response puts to rest any fears Ruth's daring approach may have aroused. In addition to his positive naming of Ruth, he provides an evaluative interpretation for her behavior by calling it a "second deed of חסד." Ruth's first deed of חסד was her refusal to abandon Naomi and her decision to abandon the land of her kindred instead. The second deed of חסד, though ostensibly affecting Boaz, is also aimed at Naomi. The two women are doomed without economic security, and Boaz as a redeemer will provide Naomi, as well as Ruth, with this security.

4.3.3.7 Although the chapter contains numerous references to sexuality and fertility, the allusions are not to a romantic enterprise but rather to a business one. Ruth makes a bid for economic security and seeks legal recourse to accomplish her intention. Boaz responds positively but in the next sentence reorients Ruth and the listener to an unforeseen possibility. Someone has the right to redeem before Boaz. This reorientation introduces renewed tension, since the outcome becomes less certain.

4.3.3.8 The scene on the threshing floor concludes with Ruth again the subject of the action, that of "lying down." She does this on Boaz' advice. We may surmise that knowledge of the evening's escapade would hinder the transactions which he has in mind. Boaz' last action is to give Ruth grain. Foresight and provisions provide a prelude of things to come.

4.3.4 *Resolution (vv. 16-17)*
4.3.4.1 The resolution consists of a brief exchange between Naomi and Ruth. Ruth's last words concern Naomi. The grain was given to her by Boaz, she says, because he said "you shall not go empty (ריקם) to your mother-in-law." The words recall Naomi's reference to herself as "empty" (ריקם) on her return to Bethlehem (1:21). Whether Boaz actually spoke these words to Ruth or not, obviously Ruth is concerned about Naomi's emptiness. One may find confirmation here that Ruth's חסד in the first instance goes out toward Naomi. Finally, her words foreshadow the ultimate redemption of Naomi's emptiness through Ruth's son.

4.3.4.2 Naomi has the last word in the chapter, as she had the first. Again, she counsels Ruth, this time to passivity since the wait for matters to be completed will not be long. The chapter ends with the word "today," a sign that the tempo is speeding up. Although the final resolution to the story is yet to come, the crucial acceptance of responsibility of the two women toward each other has found satisfactory completion at the end of ch. 3.

4.4 The Counter-type-scene

4.4.1 A counter-type-scene may be found in the overall structure of Ruth (Williams: 84-85). Within this overall structure, ch. 3 presents a complete counter-type-scene itself. 1. Having already traveled to a foreign land, the female encounters the male who is the candidate for marriage. This encounter is planned by a second female. 2. The encounter takes place on the threshing floor, a substitute symbol of fertility. The woman's dress points to sexuality, as do the verbs for lying down, uncovering, spending the night, and knowing. 3. Although Ruth's act does not involve deception, there is a motif of hiding and cleverness. 4. The gift of grain symbolizes the life that is to follow. Significantly this gift is passed on by Ruth to Naomi, as she will later pass on to Naomi the gift of life (her son). 5. The woman, Ruth, leaves the place of the encounter and announces the success of the encounter to another woman.

4.4.2 All too often the story of Ruth is viewed as an idyll or a romance, a peaceful story. Yet the concern of the story is not with romance and the setting is far from peaceful. Deprivation of sustenance, lack of security, and loss of life define the context of these women. Ruth's concern is to restore these necessities, and she mediates them to Naomi who plans the essential alliance with Boaz to that end. Her gleaning provides their immediate sustenance. In ch. 3 Ruth acts on Naomi's plan with dexterity and wit, and in the end, she gives life to Naomi's empty lap. That the necessities could be provided only by a fortuitous marriage reflects the limitations of the time and the culture in which the story takes place. It must be noted, however, that Ruth's marriage does not sever her alliance with Naomi, who is the first to benefit both by the sale of her land and the gift of Ruth's son.

4.4.3 The alliance formed between Ruth and Naomi on Ruth's initiative makes this book unique. Such an alliance was and is not easily formed and maintained. Ruth gives Naomi in turn: presence, food, more food, and finally new life. The turning point in the story comes in ch. 3, when Naomi presents Ruth with a plan. Not until the alliance becomes reciprocal can Ruth make her final and best move. Ruth may be one of the first characters in literature to show what an alliance between women can accomplish.

WORKS CONSULTED

Ahlström, G. W.
    1977   "Judges 5:20f. and History." *JNES* 36:287-88.

Alonso-Schökel, L.
    1961   "Erzählkunst im Buche der Richter." *Biblica* 42:143-73.

Alter, Robert
    1981   *The Art of Biblical Narrative.* New York: Basic Books.

Astour, Michael
    1966   "Tamar the Hierodule: An Essay in the Method of Vestigial Motifs." *JBL* 85:185-96.

Bal, Mieke, Fokkelien van Dijk Hemmes, and Grietje van Ginneken
    1984   *En Sara In Haar Tent Lachte.* Utrecht: Hes Uitgevers.

Bar-Efrat, Shimeon
    1980   "Some Observations on the Analysis of Structure in Biblical Narrative." *VT* 30: 154-73.

Beattie, D. R. G.
    1974   "The Book of Ruth as Evidence for Israelite Legal Practice." *VT* 24:251-67.

Berlin, Adele
    1983   *Poetics And Interpretation of Biblical Narrative.* Sheffield: Almond Press.

Boling, Robert G.
    1975   *Judges.* Anchor Bible, 6A. New York: Doubleday.

Burney, C. F.
    1903, 1918   *The Book of Judges.* Prolegomenon by W. F. Albright. New York: Ktav. Repr. 1970.

Campbell, Edward F., Jr.
    1975   *Ruth.* Anchor Bible, 7. New York: Doubleday.

Cassuto, U.
    1973   "The Story of Tamar and Judah." Pp. 29-40 in *Biblical and Oriental Studies*, I. Jerusalem: Magnes.

Coats, George W.
    1972   "Widows' Rights: A Crux in the Structure of Genesis 38." *CBQ* 34:461-66.
    1974   "Redactional Unity in Genesis 37-50." *JBL* 93:15-21.

Crossfield, B.
    1973   "A Critical Note on Judges 4,21." *ZAW* 85:348-51.

Davies, Eryl W.
    1981   "Inheritance Rights and the Hebrew Levirate Marriage." *VT* 31:138-44 and 257-68.

Emerton, J. A.
    1975   "Some Problems in Gen 38." *VT* 25:338-61.
    1976   "An Examination of a Recent Structuralist Interpretation of Genesis xxxviii." *VT* 26:79-98.
    1979   "Judah and Tamar." *VT* 29:403-15.

Fensham, F. C.
    1964   "Did a Treaty Between the Israelites and the Kenites Exist?" *BASOR* 175:51-54.

Fuchs, Esther
    1985a   "The Literary Characterization of Mothers and Sexual Politics in the Hebrew Bible." Pp. 117-36 in *Feminist Perspectives on Biblical Scholarship.* Ed. Adela Yarbro Collins. Chico, CA: Scholars Press.
    1985b   "Who is Hiding the Truth?" Pp. 137-44 in *Feminist Perspectives on Biblical Scholarship.* Ed. Adela Yarbro Collins. Chico, CA: Scholars Press.

Globe, Alexander
    1975   "Judges v, 27." *VT* 25:362-67.

Glueck, Nelson
    1967   *Ḥesed In The Bible.* Trans. Alfred Gottschalk. Cincinnati: Hebrew Union College Press.

Goldin, Judah
    1977   "The Youngest Son, or Where does Genesis 38 Belong?" *JBL* 96:27-44.

Green, Barbara
    1982   "The Plot of the Biblical Story of Ruth." *JSOT* 23:55-68.

Gunkel, Hermann
    1913   "Ruth." Pp. 65-92 in *Reden und Aufsätze.* Göttingen: Vandenhoeck & Ruprecht.

Hals, Ronald M.
    1969   *The Theology of the Book of Ruth.* Philadelphia: Fortress.

Hauser, Alan J.
    1980   "Judges 5: Parataxis in Hebrew Poetry." *JBL* 99:23-41.

Lagrange, Marie-Joseph
    1903   *Le Livre des Juges.* Études Bibliques. Paris: Librairie Victor Lecoffre.

Langland, Elizabeth and Walter Gove, eds.
    1981   *A Feminist Perspective in the Academy: The Difference It Makes.* Chicago: University of Chicago Press.

Malamat, A.
    1962   "Mari and the Bible." *JAOS* 82:143-50.

Moore, George F.
    1895   *A Critical and Exegetical Commentary on Judges.* Edinburgh: T & T Clark.

Murray, D. F.
    1979   "Narrative Structure and Technique in the Deborah-Barak Story (Judges 4:4-22)." Pp. 154-83 in *Studies in the Historical Books of the Old Testament*. Ed. J. A. Emerton. VTS 30. Leiden: E. J. Brill.

Nicholson, E. W.
    1977   "The Problem of צנה." ZAW 89:259-66.

Rauber, D. F.
    1970   "Literary Values in the Bible: The Book of Ruth." *JBL* 89: 27-37.

Rowley, Harold H.
    1952   "The Marriage of Ruth." Pp. 163-86 in *The Servant of the Lord and Other Essays on the Old Testament*. London: Lutterworth.

Soggin, J. A.
    1981a   "Heber der Qenit." *VT* 31:89-92.
    1981b   *Judges: A Commentary*. The Old Testament Library. Philadelphia: Westminster.

Spacks, Patricia Meyer
    1981   "The Difference it Makes," Pp. 7-24 in *A Feminist Perspective in the Academy: The Difference it Makes*. Ed. Elizabeth Langland and Walter Gove. Chicago: University of Chicago Press.

Sternberg, Meir
    1985   *The Poetics of Biblical Narrative: Ideological Literature and the Drama of Reading*. Bloomington: Indiana University Press.

Taylor, J. Glen
    1982   "The Song of Deborah and Two Canaanite Goddesses." *JSOT* 23:99-108.

Thompson, Thomas and Dorothy
    1968   "Some Legal Problems in the Book of Ruth." *VT* 18:79-99.

Trible, Phyllis
    1978   *God and the Rhetoric of Sexuality*. Philadelphia: Fortress.

"FOR I HAVE THE WAY OF WOMEN": DECEPTION, GENDER, AND IDEOLOGY IN BIBLICAL NARRATIVE

Esther Fuchs
The University of Arizona

ABSTRACT

This article suggests that gender is a primary factor which determines the literary presentation of deception in the biblical narrative. Focusing on Genesis 31, I offer a comparative study of the presentation of Rachel vis-à-vis Jacob and Laban. The results point to three major strategies which appear to distinguish Rachel's presentation: the suppression of motivation, insufficient indices of authorial judgment, the absence of a confrontational paradigm and consequently the lack of closure. That such permanent narrative gaps rarely appear in the literary presentation of male protagonists suggests that a gender-blind literary approach to the biblical text is liable to perpetuate the sexual-political status quo implied by the biblical text. By insisting on the patriarchal functions of the biblical representation of female deception, this article offers a rationale and methods for reevaluating the claim to objectivity of literary biblical scholarship.

> Women's honor, something altogether else: virginity, chastity, fidelity to a husband. Honesty in women has not been considered important. We have been depicted as generically whimsical, deceitful, subtle, vacillating. And we have been rewarded for lying.
> Adrienne Rich

0.1 Lying is the intentional prevarication of facts through the manipulation of language. Deception is the intentional production of (a) misleading message(s)—through linguistic or other means—or the intentional concealment of required information. The concept of deception is predicated upon the expected correspondence of semiosis and reality, language and fact. To deceive is to signify something to which no real state of things corresponds. Semioticians like Umberto Eco are right in emphasizing the interdependence of deception and the process of signification (58-59). But the focus on the mechanics of deception often ignores its political aspect, or the power relations between addresser and addressee. This aspect will be at the center of the following analysis of the literary presentation of deceptive women in the biblical narrative.

0.2 At the risk of oversimplifying the complex relationship of language and patriarchal authority, I will offer the following generalizations as my preliminary hypotheses. Patriarchal ideology does not differ from other hegemonic ideologies in its dependence on the control of the production and consumption of signs, or what we might call the semiotic economy. To understand what Mary Daly calls the "deadly deception" of patriarchal thinking and "metapatriarchal" thinking which often poses as scholarly analysis (43-50), it is essential to examine the relationship of women and language. For as the symbolic interpretation/representation of reality, language also has the power to determine or constitute reality and/or truth. It should therefore not surprise us that denying women access to language and depicting them as deceitful have been among the most successful strategies of traditional patriarchies.

0.3 This may explain the frequent association of women and deception in the Hebrew Bible (Fuchs, 1985b). Few scholars have noted the peculiar relationship of women and language in the Hebrew Bible, and even fewer have considered the role of heterosexual politics in this relationship. James G. Williams suggests that: "The mediating function of the feminine in many symbolic texts and contexts [in the Hebrew Bible] is closely related to the function of language, that of mediating self and world to each other" (119). But if the function of language and the feminine is to mediate between self and world, we might conclude that the feminine (and, for that matter, language) is neither (in) the self nor (in) the world but rather somewhere in between. Williams does not ask what might be the political/ideological function of such localization. The failure to bring out the political aspect of the troublesome relationship of language and women in the Hebrew Bible risks mystifying and validating this relationship.

0.4 In what follows, I would like to develop what I began to ask in a largely exploratory way about the political and ideological aspects of female characterization in the biblical narrative in general (Fuchs, 1982; 1985a) and about female deceptiveness in the Hebrew Bible in particular (Fuchs, 1985b). In "Who is Hiding the Truth? Deceptive

Women and Biblical Androcentrism," I argued for an awareness of the relationship between the patriarchal factor and the frequent presentation of women as deceptive. Addressing a variety of deceptive images, I suggested that there is a difference between the representation of male and female deceptiveness, a difference directly related to biblical patriarchal politics. Here, I would like to develop and refine this argument by focusing on a single case study, Rachel's deception of Laban and Jacob in Genesis 31:19-36, and the political implications of its structural and ideological relationship to Jacob's and Laban's deceptiveness.

1.1 The story of Rachel's deception dramatizes what I think distinguishes biblical tales of female deception: *the suppression of explicit indices of motivation, the suspension of authorial judgment, and the absence of closure.* As we shall see, these literary strategies create the impression that deceptiveness is somehow generic to women. By suppressing motivation, the narrator makes it difficult for the reader to exonerate the female deceiver. By suspending judgment, the narrator creates a kind of ambiguity which may lead to a paleosymbolic association of femininity and deceptiveness. The absence of closure contributes to this vagueness, suggesting that in the case of women, deception is not a problem requiring punishment or reformation. In our particular case study, the association of deception and menstruation permits a more intricate and refined analysis of the possible connections between the narrative gaps typical of the biblical representation of female deception, and the tendency of phallocentric language to either deny or demean female experience. In a way, the dismissal of female experience as deception is necessary for the perpetuation of the hegemony of patriarchal semiosis.

1.2 In several important ways, ch. 31 presents a closure to the deceptive treatment of Jacob by Laban (Gen 29:19-30; 30:25-34), which presents in its turn a closure to the deceptive treatment of Esau by Jacob (Gen 25:29-34; 27:1-42). Genesis 31 marks the conclusion as well of Laban's deceptive exploitation of his daughters and his son-in-law. Just as Jacob is punished through deception, so Laban is punished through deception. Laban's תרפים, or idols, are stolen by Rachel (Gen 31:19), who proceeds to feign ignorance about their whereabouts in response to her father's attempt to find them (vv. 34-35). Chapter 31 also puts in the mouths of Jacob and Laban, the male antagonists, harsh mutual reprimands that function as implicit judgments of their actions (vv. 26-30,36-42). Each antagonist has a chance to explain his deceptive actions (vv. 31-32,43-44) and finally the tense relationship between the two comes to some resolution through a mutual covenant (ברית), and a public ceremony signifying a new compromise and friendship between them (vv. 45-54). This celebratory closure highlights by contrast the open-ended nature of Rachel's characterization. She is neither punished nor reprimanded for her deceptiveness. Her actions are reported with few if any motivational or evaluative indices. Consequently, Rachel's deceptiveness fails to be shown as problematic or to be resolved in the way Jacob's or Laban's deceptiveness is.

1.3 Rachel's deception of her father (Gen 31:35) is presented as the necessary outcome of her unmotivated stealing of her father's idols. The verse reporting the theft is not preceded by any explanation. Positioned as it is between two verses referring to Jacob's departure, the verse appears to disrupt the narrative flow: "Laban had gone to shear his sheep, and Rachel stole her father's idols" (Gen 31:19). The temporal clause whose subject is Laban explains *how* it was possible for Rachel to steal rather than *why* she decided to steal the idols. Laban's temporary absense from his tent explains how Rachel managed to steal his idols. Explicitly, the function of the temporal clause of v. 19 is descriptive rather than causal, circumstantial rather than psychological. It does not provide us with an insight into Rachel's mind, or what we might call her inner world. What the syntactic combination of Laban and Rachel may suggest, however, is that being the daughter of a deceiver, Rachel has inherited his fundamental characteristic. The syntactic combination of Laban's shearing (לגזז) his sheep and Rachel's stealing (ותגנב) the idols may also suggest that the actions are in some way related. For enjoying the stolen product of Jacob's labor, Laban is punished by having something of value stolen from him by none other than his own daughter. For all these possible implications, our original question regarding Rachel's motivations remains unanswered. For we do not know whether Rachel values the idols themselves, or whether she uses them to take vengeance on Laban.

1.4 One may argue that the opaqueness of Rachel's characterization only illustrates the general tendency of the biblical narrator to maintain varying degrees of reticence or ambiguity in his characterizations (e.g. Alter: 114-30). Yet, in morally problematic contexts, such reticence is very rare (Bar Efrat: 89-112; 199-235; Sternberg, 1985: 186-221). Or rather, as I shall show here, the suspension of authorial judgment is especially rare where important male characters are concerned. The biblical narrator may be indirect or subtle in his characterization and evaluation of male protagonists caught in compromising situations, but he is rarely as reticent as he tends to be with their female counterparts. While it is true that narrative gapping and ambiguity are among the major literary hallmarks of the biblical text, I find important differences in the degree and extent of narrative reticence between accounts of male versus female deception.

2.1   The permanent gaps surrounding Rachel's deception stand out all the more prominently by contrast with the detailed presentations of Jacob's and Laban's motivations. The lengthy monologue Jacob addresses to his wives prior to Rachel's theft functions as only one of a series of implicit justifications for Jacob's stealthy abdication (Gen 31:5-13). In terms of pure information, there is little in this monologue that was not already described with great detail in Gen 30:25-43. We already know that Jacob was successful thanks to Yhwh's intervention on his behalf. We already know about the striped, mottled, and spotted sheep and goats. We even know from Gen 31:3 that God enjoined Jacob to return to Canaan. Why repeat all this information in Jacob's monologue to his wives? It seems to me that the answer lies in Jacob's numerous references to אלהים, אל (Gen 31:7,9,11,13) as the author of his success, and the reason for his wish to return to Canaan. In his monologue Jacob presents God as the one who conceived of the successful sheep breeding enterprise (vv. 8-12). From the monologue we also learn that Jacob does not merely wish to depart for Canaan because he has become wealthy and economically independent, but because God enjoins him to do so.

2.2   What Jacob's monologue significantly precludes is any hint at vindictiveness. The text indicates that Jacob is apprehensive about Laban, for the latter changed his attitude איננו עמו כתמול שלשום (v. 2). Jacob mentions Laban's deceptive and exploitative treatment without bitterness. What he is stressing in his address to his wives is not his victimization by their father, but his victory through God's interference. "And your father has cheated (התל) me, and changed my wages ten times, but God did not allow him to harm me" (31:7). Jacob's gratitude for God's protection seems to override what might or perhaps should have induced him to retaliate against Laban. By contrast, Rachel's and Leah's response is informed by vindictiveness, as they stress their economic deprivation by their father. Only the last verse of their response contains a reference to God: "And Rachel and Leah answered and said to him: Is there still for us any portion or inheritance in our father's house? For indeed we are considered by him as foreigners, for he has sold us and he has used up the money given for us. All the riches that Elohim took away from our father is ours and our sons', and now all that God told you, do" (31:14-16).

2.3   While Jacob implies that all his possessions belong in fact to God, Rachel and Leah—presented here as speaking with one voice and mind—feel that the property God took away from Laban belongs to them. Whereas Jacob emphasizes God in his monologue, his wives stress the financial aspect as their primary concern. Their references to portion (חלק), inheritance (נחלה), selling (מכרנו), money (כספנו), riches

(עשׁר) brings out the sisters' motives for renouncing their father. It is noteworthy that Rachel and Leah are quoted as complaining about their own rather than their husband's victimization by Laban. Whereas Jacob's statement about Laban's cheating him is substantiated by the omniscient narrator in previous passages (Gen 29:22-26, 27-30), the sisters' complaints are nowhere substantiated. Furthermore, since previous marital accounts (e.g. Rebekah's, Gen 24:50-67) suggest that a bride's father could indeed use the money he received in return for his daughter, we are left wondering about the validity of Rachel's and Leah's complaint. A case might be made that the narrator is in fact satirizing Rachel and Leah for complaining so strenuously about Laban's trickery and opportunism, when both colluded in a transaction that involved spending the night with Jacob. Coming from Rachel, who sold Leah the pleasure of spending the night with Jacob in return for Reuben's mandrakes (Gen 30:14-16), the daughters' self-righteous accusation of their father works as a kind of irony of self betrayal. But perhaps most significant is the fact that while Jacob's monologue refers to God's injunction as his primary motivation, the sisters' response stresses the financial aspect and Laban's exploitativeness as the primary justifications for departure. Jacob's wives urge him to "do" (עשׂה) as God told him, only after enumerating the practical reasons for doing so. In this fashion, the narrator transfers to Rachel and Leah the motivations which might have shed an ambiguous light on Jacob's flight.

3.1 The dialogue between Jacob and his wives fulfills several functions. It exonerates Jacob from Laban's subsequent accusation to the effect that the latter kidnapped his daughters and carried them away like "captives of the sword" (כשׁביות חרב v. 26). It exonerates Jacob from the (reader's) potential suspicion that his return to Canaan is induced by financial rather than religious motives. This is done by projecting the financial set of motives onto Leah and Rachel and denying their existence in Jacob's mind. By setting up a contrast between Jacob's piety on the one hand and the sisters' pragmatic reasoning (and Rachel's deceptiveness and vindictiveness) on the other, the narrator dramatizes Jacob's transformation from a deceptive opportunist into a God-fearing man. The response, and the actions attributed to Rachel, dramatize wherein lies the difference between the young Jacob and the older Jacob. The words and actions attributed to the sisters, but primarily to Rachel, signal a subtle transference of the will and ability to deceive from Jacob to his wife(wives).

3.2.1 The singular form of the verb ענה and the fact that Rachel precedes Leah as the subject of v. 14 suggests that Rachel was the primary respondent, and that Leah merely consented with or followed her sister's initiative.¹ But if we can safely argue that Rachel is the primary respondent, and consequently that the bitterness and vindictiveness the verse reflects may be attributed primarily to Rachel, we are still left with the question why. That is, why does the narrator prefer to present Rachel rather than Leah as her father's primary adversary? Why is it Rachel rather than Leah who is shown to steal Laban's idols?

3.2.2   A possible answer to the last question is that having Rachel steal Laban's idols dramatizes more vividly the *lex talionis* principle which controls the Jacob cycle. For it was Rachel whom Laban stole from Jacob, when the latter came to ask for her in return for his seven years' labor (Gen 29:20-23). It is therefore all the more fitting to present Rachel, the object of Jacob's desire, as the one who steals from her father his own objects of desire.

3.3   But Laban's punishment through Rachel is only one paradigm at work in Jacob's cycle. As Michael Fishbane has pointed out, the larger purpose of the mirror structure of the cycle is to "give Jacob his comeuppance and circumspectly redress the injustice of his original act of deceit" (55). *Rachel is the answer for the somewhat conflicting needs of these two paradigms. By having Rachel steal Laban's idols, the narrator penalizes Laban without unduly involving Jacob in yet another compromising situation. In this fashion the narrator demonstrates that the swindler (Laban) received his just deserts, while at the same time showing that Jacob has become fully reformed in Aram and is ready to return to Canaan.*

3.4   The use of the verb גנב in reference to both Rachel's and Jacob's actions first suggests an analogy between them: "And Rachel stole (ותגנב) her father's idols. And Jacob stole (ויגנב) the heart of Laban the Aramean in that he did not tell him that he was about to flee (ברח)" (31:19-20). This apparent analogy, however, only highlights the important differences between the actions designated by the homologous verb גנב. For one thing, the literal use of גנב in reference to Rachel and its figurative use in reference to Jacob indicates that while Rachel committed an actual theft, Jacob "stole" in a manner of speaking, that is, idiomatically. That Jacob did not steal anything from Laban is made clear in the detailed description of his work, and the detailed explanation for his economic success (Gen 29:20-21,27-28; 30:26-43; 31:5-12). Verses 17 and 18, which describe Jacob's preparations for the journey, implicitly repeat that Jacob's belongings are lawfully his own by insist-

---

¹ Compare the use of the singular verb in reference to Deborah and Barak in Judges 5:1.

ing on the use of the third person possessive "his": "And Jacob arose, and set *his* sons and *his* wives on camels, and he drove away all *his* cattle, all *his* livestock *which he has gained*, the cattle *in his possession which he gained in Paddan-Aram*, to go to the land of Canaan to his father Isaac." Lest we miss the implications of the possessive, the repeated relative clause אשר רכש challenges any doubt we may have about Jacob's lawful claim to the property he took away with him from Paddan-Aram.

3.5 The juxtaposition of Jacob's figurative גנב and Rachel's literal גנב suggests both similarity and contrast. Both succeed in deceiving Laban, but whereas Jacob's deception is presented as an act of self-defense, Rachel's unexplained deception seems arbitrary. Laban, who is unaware of his daughter's deception, emerges from his confrontational scene with Jacob as the victim of dramatic irony. For as Laban is accusing Jacob of deception and of mistreating his daughters, the reader is aware that it is precisely the objects of his concern that betrayed Laban most severely. Laban accuses Jacob of "carrying away" (נהג) his daughters as "captives of the sword" (v. 26), and of depriving him of the opportunity to kiss his daughters and sons goodbye (v. 28), while we know that his daughters left willingly and had little interest in taking a ceremonious leave of their father (vv. 15-16). Laban uses the verb גנב three times, twice in the figurative sense of cheating (vv. 26-27), and once in the literal sense "and you stole my gods" (v. 30). The glaring mistake Laban makes in attributing to Jacob the stealing of the gods reflects his attributing exclusively to Jacob the interest in the stealthy flight. Ultimately, Laban is deceived by his misperception of Jacob and of his daughters. His (alleged) trust in his daughters and (overt) distrust of Jacob are just as misguided as his valuation of his idols.

3.6 By juxtaposing Jacob's figurative גנב with Rachel's literal גנב the text implies that Jacob's deception is not as grave. Not only does the text provide him with more substantive and detailed reasons for stealing away from his father-in-law, there is also the element of kinship. Rachel is more closely related to Laban than Jacob. This increases the objectionableness of her deceptiveness. Yet, it is Jacob rather than Rachel who is provided with both a preliminary and a retrospective justification for stealing Laban's heart. The preliminary justification (31:1-13) makes it clear that Jacob wishes to leave for Canaan because he is tired of being exploited and deceived (vv. 7-10), because Laban has begun to treat him even worse (vv. 1-2,5), and because God ordered him to return to Canaan (vv. 11-13). The retrospective justification is put in Jacob's mouth in response to Laban's furious questions about Jacob's stealthy departure: "Because I was afraid, for I thought (אמר) that you would take by force (גזל) your daughters away from me" (v. 31).

4.1 Jacob's fear is understandable in light of Laban's deceptive manipulation of his fatherly authority in the past (Gen 29:23-27). Jacob's perceived need to deceive his foe for fear of losing his wives reminds us of Abram-Abraham's deception of the Egyptian Pharaoh (Gen 12:10-20) and of Abimelech the king of Gerar (Gen 20) for fear of losing his life on account of his attractive wife. It also reminds us that Isaac deceived Abimelech for the same reason: "For I thought that I might die on her account" (Gen 26:9). Like his predecessors, Jacob resorts to deception because of a perceived fear associated with his wives. But perhaps more significantly, Jacob is challenged by Laban, just as Abraham and Isaac are confronted by their respective competitors. This confrontation allows all three heroes to explain their actions, which constitutes the prelude to an agreement of peace with their adversaries, and thereby to some kind of moral closure. But as already noted, Jacob is even more justified than Abraham and Isaac in opting for the deception at this point, in view of his bitter experience of Laban's dishonesty in the past.

4.2 Were Rachel said to steal or deceive for fear, her action may not have seemed as objectionable, not only because the specification of motivation is likely to mitigate the negative implications of an act of deception but also because one's fear of a politically superior party often emerges as the most acceptable prelude to deceptive strategies in the biblical text. When used as a means of self-defense, deception emerges often not only as an understandable ploy but also as a necessary, and even venerable ploy (e.g. Ehud's deception of Eglon, Yael's deception of Sisera). In the case of Sarah's deceptive denial concerning her incredulous laughter in response to God's promise of progeny, the text specifies that she "lied" (כחש), "because she was afraid" (Gen 18:15). Sarah's faithlessness and her false denial does not add much to her moral stature, yet, by explaining it, the text mitigates its negativity. Rebekah's deception of Esau and Isaac is more problematic and complex than Sarah's deception. As I have noted elsewhere, the text does not make us aware of the constraints of patriarchal order which in some ways offer deception as the only alternative for a mother interested in the welfare of a particular child (Fuchs, 1985b: 138). Nevertheless, the text points to at least two justifications for her questionable actions: the divine oracle preceding the birth of her twins (Gen 25:23), and her love for Jacob (Gen 25:28). Yet unlike Abraham and Isaac, their male counterparts, Sarah and Rebekah do not benefit from the moral closure we noted above. And unlike Sarah and Rebekah, Rachel can not be said to have been motivated by fear, love, or faith in God. Nor can her deception of her father be perceived as an expression of loyalty to her husband, as we might construe, for example, Michal's deception of Saul (2 Sam 18:13-17). The fact that Rachel is shown to act on her own, and that Jacob is so incensed by the theft as to curse the thief, indicates that Rachel did not necessarily act in Jacob's interests (Gen 31:32).

4.3 The suppression of information about Rachel's motives leaves us with several problematic possibilities. Her theft could be construed as the result of greed, presuming that the idols are monetarily valuable. It could be construed as an act of spite, motivated by filial disobedience and vindictiveness, which is perhaps the most acceptable possibility. Her theft could, however, also be read as the result of an idolatrous inclination, as we may assume that Rachel is personally attached to her father's household idols and does not wish to part with them. The potential of these possibilities to cast Rachel's already weak moral stature in an even more negative light, reveals with great clarity the need for the confrontational paradigm and the structural closure that we observed in the stories of the patriarchs' deception. The absence of these paradigms brings out the significant differences between tales of male and female deception in the Hebrew Bible.

4.4 By letting Jacob explain his motives for stealing away with his wives and property, the narrator validates Jacob's actions. To insure his complete exoneration, the narrator does not allow us to speculate whether or not Jacob colluded with Rachel. For these purposes, the narrator makes use of his omniscient stance, offering us a direct glimpse into Jacob's mind: "And Jacob did not know (לא ידע) that Rachel stole them [the idols]" (Gen 31:32). By fully explaining Jacob's motives for stealing away from Laban, and by clarifying that—unlike Rachel's deception—this move was strategically necessary (v. 31), the narrator removes any doubt we might entertain about Jacob's moral reformation. The authorial intrusion clarifying that Jacob was unaware of his wife's crime not only makes clear that he curses her unintentionally, but also that he is outraged by the act, and that had he known, he would have tried either to prevent it or to make amends. Ambiguity is not something the narrator can afford at this important juncture in the narrative, whose goal is to dramatize Jacob's moral transition from a cunning Ya'akov to an upright Israel.

5.1 In view of the variety and complexity of the strategies the narrator employs in conjunction with the characterization and validation of Jacob, it is untenable to argue that the permanent gaps typifying Rachel's presentation are symptomatic of the biblical art of authorial reticence. Neither will it do to explain the narrative gaps by appealing to Rachel's secondary status. For one thing, this explanation begs the question: how do we explain the secondary status of the Israelite matriarch? Secondly, Laban's essentially secondary status does not preclude the attribution to him of a rather lengthy diatribe (31:26-30) as well as conciliatory speeches (vv. 43-44; 48-53), which help mitigate the negative implications of his deceptive machinations.

5.2   The differences between the literary representation of Rachel on the one hand and of her male counterparts on the other suggest that gender is a sorely overlooked factor in what has come to be known as biblical poetics. What determines the usual shuttle of the biblical narrator between what Meir Sternberg calls "the truth and the whole truth" (1979:129-133) is not only the Bible's monotheistic ideology, but also its patriarchal ideology. The irreducible differences between the temporary gaps typifying male deception and the permanent gaps, the relentless ambiguity and the lack of closure typical of female deception, are indicative of a patriarchal conception of femaleness. This conception fails to problematize moral attitudes that it tends to problematize in the case of major and secondary male characters. The textual failure to problematize, challenge, and resolve the moral ambiguity attributed to female characters reflects an epistemological economy which predicates moral judgment on a character's sexual identity. According to Judith Ochshorn, the interdependence of gender and morality distinguishes biblical monotheism from earlier polytheistic ideologies which predominated in the ancient Near East (133-236). But whether the moral devaluation of femaleness is inseparable from the Bible's monotheistic ideology or not, the fact remains that gender does constitute an irrepressible factor in biblical representations and interpretations of female deceptiveness.

6.1   As in the scene describing her stealing of the idols, so in the scene describing her encounter with Laban, we are left in the dark as to Rachel's motives. Her actions and speech do not explain or justify her deception, but rather constitute her deception:

> And Rachel had taken the idols and put them in the camel's cushion, and sat upon them. And she said to her father: "Let not my lord be angry that I cannot rise before you, for I have the way of women." So he searched, but did not find the idols (Gen 31:34-35).

As an extension and complement of the *lex talionis* paradigm which I discussed earlier, this scene punishes Laban in two complementary ways: on the one hand, the deceiver is deceived, the exploitative father is being deceptively exploited by his own daughter. On the other hand, the idols, symbolic of Laban's idolatrous beliefs (beliefs that implicitly explain his greed, deceptiveness, and relentless exploitation) are being desecrated. For not only does Rachel sit on the idols, she sits on them in a state of, what Nahum Sarna calls "menstrual impurity" (201). Those who tend to take Rachel's excuse at face value, however, tend to forget that Rachel may be appealing to "the way of women" as a deceptive excuse for keeping the idols hidden. Once again, by opting for ambiguity, the narrator avoids giving us any clues for judging the character. The permanent narrative gaps left open by the narrator make it possible for us to interpret the textual evidence as an ironic jibe against Rachel as much as against Laban, as we shall see later.

6.2 One wonders in this context, why the narrator prefers to provide us with a somewhat detailed description of Rachel's alleged actions and words in a way that he deemed unnecessary in the scene describing the theft of the idols. Just as he simply claimed that Rachel stole the idols, he could also briefly state that she hid them. But the narrator prefers to describe in some detail just *how* Rachel concealed the idols (v. 34), and how she concealed the fact that she concealed them (v. 35). The accidental concealment described in v. 34 parallels the verbal concealment quoted in v. 35. Both verses begin with a combined sentence whose subject is Rachel, followed by a consecutive sentence whose subject is Laban. The success of Rachel's deceptive act is expressed through the compact string of the three verbs לקחה ותשמם ותשב and the rhetorical persuasiveness of her polite and conciliatory tone, as well as through the repeated reference to Laban's failure to find his idols (vv. 34,35). Yet while vv. 34 and 35 represent two versions of concealment, they also create a vivid contrast between Rachel's actions and words. Rachel's actions are expressive of agility and initiative, whereas her description of herself insists on her passivity and vulnerability. Thus Rachel's deception consists in her concealment of the "real" state of things, not only in regard to the idols' whereabouts, but also in regard to her own "real" state.

6.3 Yet this relatively detailed dramatization of Rachel's deception does not clarify to what extent Rachel's appeal to her menstrual period correlates with her "real" state. The text does not clarify whether Rachel's appeal to her menstrual period is a lie, or whether she uses the fact as a convenient excuse. By leaving it open to our conjecture, the narrator is enabling us to interpret "the way of women" as a reference to Rachel's menstruation as well as to the fact that she is deceiving her father. The reader knows that Rachel does not rise before her father because his idols are hidden beneath her seat, because, in other words, she is deceiving him. The ambiguity of the described deception enables the narrator to use the powerful dramatic irony generated by this scene as a double-edged weapon against Rachel as well as Laban. For

Rachel's appeal to her "way of women" (דרך נשים) puts in her mouth a condemnation of her own sex, by combining in the same expression a reference to woman's alleged somatic impurity and moral inferiority.

6.4 The euphemistic expression which enables the linkage of female deception and menstruation is itself a linguistic device of concealment. "The way of women" is a euphemistic name for menstrual blood, which in a patriarchal economy is symptomatic of somatic impurity. The need for a "clean" expression testifies to the dis-ease which the referent arouses in the patriarchal mind, especially when the female subject in question is a respectable matriarch. The euphemism is expressive of the horror menstruation evokes in the male imagination, a horror encoded in the Levitical laws of *nidda* (Lev 15:19-33), as well as in the prophets' figurative use of *nidda* as a synonym for moral impurity (Ezek 36:17; Lam 1:17; 1 Chron 29:5). In some ways, it is inevitable that menstruation should be associated with deception, for the former does not exist in male reality, and it is only through moral devaluation and partial denial that patriarchal language can coopt it. If truth is the commensurability of language and reality, and if female reality is incommensurate with male reality, the former must be dismissed as nontruth, or deception.[2]

6.5 Because menstruation is unique to women, it should come as no surprise that patriarchal ideology should attempt to associate it with both deception and idolatry, the former signifying a negation of (male) word, and the latter signifying the negation of this word's divine authorization.[3] This may explain why Rachel is not challenged for deceiving both her father and, in a less blatant way, her husband. If deceptiveness is inherent in female nature, there is no more point in challenging it than there is in challenging the menstrual cycle. But if patriarchal politics cannot deny the existence of menstruation and its undeniable link to fertility and procreation, it can degrade it by defining it as impure and by legislating a series of laws to contain it. Similarly, if patriarchal politics cannot deny woman's ability to think and speak, it can contain, or warp, the relationship of women and language by minimizing and constricting female dialogue and by implying that it is metaphorically impure, or deceptive.[4]

---

[2] Compare Luce Irigaray's analysis of the phallogocentric treatment of female eros in Western civilization from Plato to Freud.

[3] For a thematic association of menstruation with female deceptiveness, see Gen 18:11-15. For a thematic association of idols with female deception, see 1 Sam 19:11-17.

[4] See Julia Kristeva on the relationship between biblical laws on somatic and dietary purity on the one hand and the biblical moral code on the other (90-108).

7.1.1 By failing to show Rachel's deceptiveness as problematic, the narrator forestalls the use of the confrontational paradigm which usually leads to resolution and closure. There is neither confrontation nor compromise between Rachel and Laban. Unlike Laban, who despite his questionable conduct is allowed to utter binding words of truth shortly before he leaves the narrative scene, Rachel's final words are deceptive. Unlike both Laban and Jacob, who are punished for their deceptiveness, Rachel is not shown to be punished, unless we interpret her death on the way from Bethel to Ephrath as a kind of divine punishment (Gen 35:16-24).

7.1.2 Such an interpretation would be problematic both for its unusual severity and because of its textual disjunction from the scene describing what is never quite presented as her crime. Rachel resurfaces in ch. 35, just as abruptly as she disappears from ch. 31. One could argue that Rachel's untimely death is a belated fulfillment of Jacob's curse: "Any one with whom you find your gods shall not live" (Gen 31:32). But close attention to the text would disclose that the object of Jacob's curse is the one who would be found out by Laban. Since the latter is not shown to find his gods with Rachel, it is a matter of speculation to attribute her death to Jacob's curse.

7.2 The ambiguity which typifies Rachel's deception typifies also what might or might not be her punishment. The emphasis in the scene on the fact that the dying Rachel is giving birth to a son (Gen 35:17) and the attention given to this baby's name (v. 18) suggest that the narrator is not so much interested in the moral relationship of Rachel's death to her deception as in the "product" of her death. Now that she has given birth to a second son, Rachel is no longer necessary for the progression of the story. Rachel "dies" at a convenient point, having fulfilled her procreative role, just as she has previously been whisked off the stage, having served as the means of Laban's punishment and as Jacob's foil. From this point of view, Rachel dies in "the way of women," just as she lived and deceived in "the way of women." It is not so much the fact that she dies in childbirth, but that she disappears just as abruptly as she was shown to "live."

7.3 The systematic differences in the biblical representation of deceptive men and women is crucial for our understanding of the interdependence of biblical poetics and the Bible's patriarchal ideology. An awareness of these differences should matter to both biblical feminologists and literary critics. For if gender is a factor in what determines the shape of the biblical text, it is misleading to refer to a general "art of the biblical narrative," or to a neutral "biblical poetics" (Alter; Sternberg, 1985). An awareness of the interdependence of heterosexual politics and biblical narrative is the first step in a feminist critique of the patriarchal claim to absolute "objective" truth. The critical failure to reevaluate the implications of the permanent narrative gaps discussed here risks validating the androcentric epistemology which made gaps possible in the first place. A failure to deal with the political aspect of female deceptiveness in the biblical narrative is both an academic and a political failure. By denying the problem, we risk justifying the continued hegemony of androcentric discourse in the biblical academy.

WORKS CONSULTED

Alter, Robert
    1981   *The Art of Biblical Narrative.* New York: Basic Books.

Bar-Efrat, Shimeon
    1979   *The Art of the Biblical Story.* Tel Aviv, Israel: Sifriat Poalim (Hebrew).

Daly, Mary
    1978   *Gyn/ecology: The Metaethics of Radical Feminism.* Boston: Beacon Press.

Eco, Umberto
    1976   *A Theory of Semiotics.* Bloomington & London: Indiana University Press.

Fishbane, Michael
    1979   *Text and Texture: Close Readings of Selected Biblical Texts.* New York: Schocken Books.

Fuchs, Esther
    1982   "Status and Role of Female Heroines in the Biblical Narrative." *Mankind Quarterly* 23/2: 149-60.
    1985a   "The Literary Characterization of Mothers and Sexual Politics in the Bible." Pp. 47-136 in *Feminist Perspectives on Biblical Scholarship.* Ed. Adela Yarbro Collins. Chico, CA: Scholars Press.
    1985b   "Who is Hiding the Truth? Deceptive Women and Biblical Androcentrism." Pp. 137-44 in *Feminist Perspectives on Biblical Scholarship.* Ed. Adela Yarbro Collins. Chico, CA: Scholars Press.

Irigaray, Luce
    1985   *Speculum of the Other Woman.* Trans. Gillian C. Gill. Ithaca, NY: Cornell University Press. [*Speculum de l'autre femme.* Paris: Editions de Minuit, 1974.]

Kristeva, Julia
    1982   *Powers of Horror: An Essay on Abjection.* Trans. Leon S. Roudiez. New York: Columbia University Press. [*Pouvoirs de l'horreur.* Paris: Editions du Seuil, 1980.]

Ochshorn, Judith
    1981   *The Female Experience and the Nature of the Divine.* Bloomington: Indiana University Press.

Rich, Adrienne
    1979   *On Lies, Secrets, and Silence: Selected Prose 1966-1978.* New York & London: W. W. Norton.

Sarna, Nahum M.
    1970   *Understanding Genesis.* New York: Schocken Books.

Sternberg, Meir
    1979   "The Truth vs. All the Truth: The Rendering of Inner Life in Biblical Narrative." *Hasifrut* 29:110-46 (Hebrew).
    1985   *The Poetics of Biblical Narrative: Ideological Literature and the Drama of Reading.* Bloomington: Indiana University Press.

Williams, James G.
    1982   *Women Recounted: Narrative Thinking and the God of Israel.* Sheffield: Almond Press.

THE DECEPTIVE GODDESS
IN ANCIENT NEAR EASTERN MYTH:
INANNA AND INARAŠ

Carole Fontaine
Andover Newton Theological School

ABSTRACT

Using folkloristic methodology, this study will show that the deceptive female characters of the Hebrew Bible have counterparts in the "goddess literature" of the surrounding cultures. There we see goddesses using deception as a strategy for obtaining desirable social goals, often on behalf of other members of the pantheon, or their sons, consorts, patron localities and groups (often symbolized by the king), or humanity at large. In addition, the deceptive goddess frequently appears in contexts which include the motifs of sexual exchange, drunkenness and feasting. This situation is found in the Hebrew Bible as well, and mirrors the stereotypic roles assigned to the female by patriarchal societies. The Sumerian Inanna in "Inanna and Enki: The Transfer of the Arts of Civilization from Eridu to Erech" attends a "banquet-contest" as the "Seeker-Hero" guest. In this type-scene, she successfully wrests the divine ordinances, the *me*, from her grandfather on behalf of her city. The Hittite Inaraš in "The Myth of Illuyankaš" acts as Helper to the Weather-god. As such, she is the host of a "banquet set-up" where she lures the Illuyankaš-dragon to its death. Parallels within the Hebrew Bible (Judg 14:10-20; Gen 19:30-38; Esth 5:4-8, 7:1-10; Ruth 3; Judith 12-13; Judg 5; 2 Sam 13) are discussed.

1.0 One of the dominant patterns of characterization for females found in the Hebrew Bible is that of the deceiver or "female trickster."[1]

---

[1] I use this term advisedly. Perusal of the trickster "literature" of traditional peoples shows that such figures are male, act as both destroyers and creators, and are often associated with animals significant to or admired by the cultures in question. Hence, it may be that "trickster"-hood is essentially a category of ambivalent male behavior.

Whether the woman in question uses deception to achieve goals approved by patriarchy (Rebekah, Tamar, Ruth, Rahab, Jael, Judith) or is depicted as a deceiver whose actions threaten the patriarchal order (Jezebel, Potiphar's wife, Dame Folly), the strategy for effective action most closely associated with woman characters in the Hebrew Bible is a morally ambivalent one. In addition, this strategy is often coupled with the motif of sexual exchange, or takes place in contexts where "Woman the Provider," associated with food, drink, and shelter, turns deceiver, thereby rendering the familiar nurturing figure suddenly dangerous to unsuspecting males who fall into her "snares." Feminist studies of such texts have suggested that this prevalent mode of characterization is advanced by patriarchy to reinforce its androcentric ideology by stereotyping women as deceivers. However, such stereotyping also reveals a "truth" about the condition of women (or any powerless, marginated group) under patriarchy: where women are debarred by status from direct action to achieve their goals without fear of reprisal, they will resort to indirect strategies such as deception, gossip, and counselling, which *are* available to those of inferior status (Lamphere; Fuchs).

2.0   Study of literature of the cultures surrounding ancient Israel shows that the motif of the female deceiver is not confined to the Hebrew Bible, and appears in the "goddess literature" of the region. However one chooses to view the nature of myth (as speculative thinking or derived from ritual, to greatly simplify the current debate), or the relation of the stories about goddesses to the lives of real women, it is clear that as literary type, the "deceptive goddess" is the divine sister of the woman trickster, and study of the one may illumine discourse about the other. This study will adopt the position that while myth in the ancient Near East may well grow up and be intimately connected to ritual practice (Gaster), it is also "speculative." That is, it attempts to resolve basic perceived conflicts through substitution of a series of mediating terms which eventually render the initial oppositions "livable" (Lévi-Strauss). Similarly, the functions of myth may range from the explanation of existing rituals or cultural features to the resolution of psychological conflicts. Myth operates on the social rather than individual level (unlike tales) and is characterized by the felt effects of its action in the hearer/reader's "present" (see the essays in the volume edited by Dundes). With regard to surface structure, myth may share many of the features observed in tales; in fact, some contend that structurally, a tale is simply a myth which has lost its ritual and communal context (see Reid's discussion). Hence, methods usually applied to the analysis of tale plot composition and characterization also yield results for mythic analysis.

2.1 The exact relation of the myths studied here to Israelite texts of a later period is a more difficult question to resolve. Students of the Hebrew Bible are aware, of course, of the numerous adaptations of ancient Near Eastern myth to be found within the pages of "Holy Scripture"—the dependence of Genesis 1 on the structure of the Enuma Elish or the relation of the Song of the Sea to the mythic patterns of the Baal cycle are prime examples. Perhaps because of the patriarchal biases intrinsic to the biblical text and engendered in its interpreters, we are less used to asking questions about biblical parallels to "goddess" texts. Even so, it has been observed, however reluctantly on the part of some, that "goddess functions" (actions performed by goddesses to advance the action in their stories) are often transferred to the Hebrew God, that god's human (male) surrogate-heroes, the people Israel, and less frequently, to Israel's women (see Taylor for transfer of Anat and Asherah functions to Deborah and Jael in Judg 5, and Sasson: 67 for Inanna's ritual activities in Ruth 3:3a).

2.11 Yhwh "inexplicably" seeks Moses' life in Exod 4:24-26 until stopped by Zipporah's sacramental action of shedding ritual blood. The pattern becomes understandable, however, once it is seen that Yhwh's behavior parallels that of the bloodthirsty Hathor (and, less so, Anat) who is deterred from further destruction by the sight of blood (Pritchard: 11). (Zipporah's action may be understood as an example of making the hero acceptable to the submerged goddess through induction of symbolic menstruation in the male hero.[2]) Similarly, in Psalm 22 Yhwh's actions in vv. 9-10 are reminiscent of the Mother-goddesses of Hittite myth who take the babe from the womb, and officiate in the naming (Hoffner), or the goddesses Isis, Nephthys, Meskhenet, and Heket who assist at birth in the Westcar Papyrus (but note the presence of the potter-god Khnum in their company, Simpson: 26). Moses utterly destroys the remains of the Golden Calf in Exod 32:20 with stereotypic actions performed by Anat in her destruction of Baal's murderer, Mot (Pritchard: 140). The people Israel (or the actual land of Israel) fill the role of the goddess if the Song of Songs is interpreted "allegorically" as a Sacred Marriage rite, and echoes of this transfer find their way into Hosea's theology (Hos 2). In a parallel to Yhwh's action against the oppressors of Egypt in Exod 7:14-25, when the goddess Inanna is raped by the gardener Shukalletuda while she sleeps beneath one of his trees, she sends a series of plagues upon the land in which the rapist is hiding. The first plague is one of blood:

---

[2] For a discussion of this phenomenon in other cultures, see Grahn: 272-73.

> All the wells of the land she filled with blood,
> All the groves and gardens of the land she sated with blood,
> The (male) slaves coming to gather firewood,
>   drink nothing but blood,
> The (female) slaves coming to fill up with water,
> fill up with nothing but blood . . . (Kramer, 1956:69).

Examples of such transfer and transformation of goddess functions within the Hebrew Bible might easily be multiplied.

2.2 The deceptive goddesses explored here do not, for the most part, offer direct syntagmatic parallels to the stories of women portrayed in the Hebrew Bible (but compare the Egyptian Tale of Two Brothers and the Hittite "El, Ashertu and the Storm-god" [Pritchard: 23-25, 519] with Gen 39 for an exception to this), but the myths and biblical texts existed in the same thought world of literary conventions. Hence, the female tricksters of the Hebrew Bible need not necessarily be viewed as survivals of the paradigmatic, degraded goddess, but neither should they be considered as isolated occurrences. Whether their actions were judged positively or negatively within a given story, patriarchy painted its female characters with a single brush. The rule of androcentrism operated both in the recitation of myths of the divine world and in the telling of tales of human ancestors, a rule from which no text originating in this region and epoch could escape entirely. With these considerations in mind, we will now examine the role of the deceptive goddess in myths from Sumer and Anatolia.

3.0 The goddess Inanna, whose name may be interpreted as "Lady of the Date Clusters" or "Queen of Heaven" (Jacobsen, 1976:36, 137), was adored in Sumer from earliest times. City-goddess of Uruk (Erech), she is daughter of the moongod Nanna and his consort Ningal, granddaughter of the god of wisdom and sweet fertilizing waters, Enki ("Lord Earth"), and full sister to the sungod Utu. The numinous power of the filled storehouse, and divine partner of the date-gatherer and later shepherd Dumuzi in the Sacred Marriage rite, the attributes given her far outdistance the simple appellation "fertility goddess." She is called "Nin-me-šar-ra," "Lady of a myriad offices," a goddess of "infinite variety," for she is not only the power of abundance felt in the overflowing larder, but the "dread storm" with its terrible, yet life-giving rains. She also appears as the goddess of the morning and evening stars (Jacobsen, 1976:135-41). Perhaps related to her function as illuminatrix of the night sky, she is also the protector of the harlot, whose way she lights. Battle itself is "the dance of Inanna" for she is goddess of war, "the heart of the battle," and "Nin-kur-ra-igi-gal," "the queen who eyes the highland," whose might is feared even in distant lands (Jacobsen,

1976:137; Kramer, 1952:10). More autonomous than her semitic counterpart Ištar, with whom she is eventually fused (Ochshorn: 24), bride and widow she may be, but "she is never depicted as a wife and helpmate or as a mother" (Jacobsen, 1976:141). Ironically, while other "mother-goddesses" were systematically demoted by Sumerian theologians in the third millenium (see 3.5 below), Inanna accrued power by means of her association with the Sacred Marriage, where her sexual union with the king in the role of Dumuzi authorized the patriarchal institution of kingship (Wakeman: 91-92).

3.1 In "Inanna and Enki: The Transfer of the Arts of Civilization from Eridu to Erech," first outlined in Kramer's *Sumerian Mythology* with translations of central passages (1972:64-68), we see her as a city-goddess *par excellence*. Here she travels to the city of her grandfather Enki and returns to Uruk with the divine ordinances, the *me*, given to her by Enki in a fit of drunken magnanimity (for a critical edition of the text, see Farber-Flügge; in English, see Wolkstein and Kramer: 12-27, where some repetitions of the lists of the *me* are omitted). Dates for this third millenium text range from the Ur III dynasty to the Isin dynasty of Iddin-Dagan for its composition (Farber-Flügge: 4-7); Kramer dates its written form to about 2000 B.C.E. (1972:66).

3.11 Our myth is one of the compositions classified as a "divine journey" text (see, for example, "Nanna-Suen's Journey to Nippur," "Enki's Journey to Nippur," "Ningirsu's Journey to Eridu," "Ninurta's Journey to Eridu," cited in Ferrara). This genre depicts a journey by a god/ess, often by boat, to a sanctuary of another, for the purpose of obtaining "a favorable destiny vis-à-vis the establishment of prosperity and abundance which the visited deity's blessing would ensure" (Ferrara: 3). More precisely defined, our text no doubt celebrates the rising fortunes of the city of Uruk and its alliance with Enki's city Eridu, as its final passages suggest. By means of its inherent "mythopoeic" thought processes, it may also attempt to explain and overcome the apparent contradiction of how the city's patron, a female "fertility" figure, at the same time could be the source of the civilizing arts for her city.[3]

3.12 Typically for the myth genre, divine action, here of the goddess Inanna who took over rule of Uruk from the heaven god An around 3000 B.C.E. (Kramer, 1974:16), is viewed as the source of the benefits of the *me* which undergird and shape the structures of human society.

---

[3] In fact, this myth nicely fits Lévi-Strauss' notorious formula, $F_x(a) : F_y(b) , F_x(b) : F_{a\text{-}1}(y)$, for mythic action (228). In Eridu (x), Enki resides with the *me* (a), while Inanna with her wondrous vulva (b) resides in Uruk (y); when Inanna (b) enters Eridu (x), Enki is deprived of the *me* (a-1), which are transferred to Uruk (y).

Usually Sumerian compositions of a mythic and epical nature show no evidence that they were associated with ritual, which suggests to some that they had as their life-setting the *edubba*, or scribal school (Kramer, 1963:169-70). However, it has been argued that some of the less combative "divine journey" texts are related to ritual journeys of divine images/emblems undertaken in the Old and Neo-Sumerian periods (Ferrara: 1-4). Nevertheless, the multiple repetitions of the list of the *me* in our text suggest a didactic life-setting as well as a ritual one (Wolkstein and Kramer: 147, n. 13).

3.13 Briefly sketched, the action of this myth proceeds as follows: rejoicing in her powers of womanhood, Inanna sets out on a quest to visit Enki's palace, the Abzu. As she nears, Enki commands his vizier Isimud to set a feast for her, to "treat her like an equal." Inanna enters and she and Enki begin to drink beer, toasting and challenging one another. "Swaying with drink," Enki toasts the goddess and begins a series of offers of groups of the *me* to Inanna. After each offer, the text reports "The pure Inanna receives (them)" (kù-^{d}inanna-ke$_4$ šu ba(-ti), Farber-Flügge: 20). This happens fourteen times until all of the *me*, from the ordinances governing high priesthood and godship to judgment-giving and decision making, have been presented to the goddess. Enki commands that Inanna be allowed to reach Uruk safely, and the goddess loads the *me* in the Boat of Heaven and sets out for her city.

3.14 Enki, upon sobering up, realizes that the *me* are gone, and questions Isimud fourteen times about their whereabouts, each time receiving the reply, "My king has given them to his daughter." Enki sends Isimud and protective, zoomorphic *enkum*-creatures after the goddess, who refuses Isimud's request to return the Boat of Heaven to Eridu. Angry at her grandfather's change of heart, Inanna dispatches her own vizier Ninshubur by means of a magic formula which suggests her (Ninshubur's) immunity to Enki. Inanna orders her to defend the *me*-laden craft, which she does successfully. Seven times, perhaps at ritual stopping points in the cultic journey, Ninshubur rescues the Boat of Heaven from Isimud and the creatures dispatched by Enki. Arriving finally at Uruk, when the Boat of Heaven is unloaded, more *me* are found aboard than were originally presented to Inanna (including the art of women, allure, the placing of the garment on the ground, and the perfect execution of the *me*). These *me*, the special "finds" of Inanna, are also given to the people of Uruk. The myth ends with Enki's reconciliation to Inanna and a declaration that the *me* are to remain in Uruk, as Eridu and Uruk become allies (Wolkstein and Kramer: 12-27).

3.2 This myth contains two *topoi* typical to the literature about Inanna: her special relationship with the god of wisdom, Enki, and her preoccupation with the *me* (Hallo and Van Dijk: 48). In "Inanna's Descent to the Underworld," it is Enki who provides the means for rescue after the gods Enlil and even father Nanna refuse to aid Inanna's Helper Ninshubur (Wolkstein and Kramer: 61-64). In another text, "Enki and the World Order," Inanna and Enki again appear together in contention over the *me*, with Inanna claiming that Enki has slighted her in his distribution of the *me* (Kramer, 1963:171-83). In "The Exaltation of Inanna" by the Sargonic princess-priestess Enheduanna, we also find Inanna hailed as the possessor of the *me*, but in this composition she has received them from the god of Heaven, An (Hallow and Van Dijk: 17), rather than from Enki, and there is no hint of deception or craft in this transaction.

3.3 From the perspective of roles played by the participants involved in the present myth, we see the literary grounds for the "character reading" usually accorded to Inanna. While it is clear that the genres of myth and tale pursue different agendas (see 2.0 above), the same cast of dramatis personae found acting in tales often appears in myth and other narrative genres influenced by principles of traditional (oral) composition, as has been amply demonstrated elsewhere. Such character roles are defined by the *actions* performed by the various players, and in tales with male heroes, seven such roles are typical: Hero, Villain, Donor (Giver), Helper, Princess (Sought-for-Person) and Her Father, Dispatcher (Sender), and False Hero (Propp: 79-83). Further refinement of the scheme delineates a set of actors present in "Innocent Persecuted Heroine" tales, though these are drawn from a much smaller sample of texts than those Propp was working through, and still await cross-cultural testing. These representative roles are: Heroine, Groom/ Husband, Heroine's Male Relatives (father, brother), Villains (male seducers, socially elder female relatives of heroine or her husband, False Bride), and Benevolent Roles (marvelous Helper, Agent, Benefactor; see Dan: 14 for discussion).

3.31 Analysis of the roles played by Inanna in the myth in question provide us with fresh insight into the characterization of this goddess. At the outset of the action, she serves as her own Donor (Giver) and Dispatcher (Sender), as she praises her womanly powers (the wondrous item which will allow the successful completion of her quest) and sends herself off to visit Enki. Enki acts first as Donor (later as Villain) in offering her the *me*. Together, as Hero and Donor, Inanna and Enki engage in a drinking contest which we understand here as a "Donor Test," the stylized encounter—sometimes hostile—through which power is redistributed from Donor to Hero. Since heroes do not always pass such "tests" successfully, the outcome of Inanna's direct action in meeting Enki's challenge to drink with him suggests that she is an entirely adequate hero and foreshadaows her final success in retaining the *me* against all comers. Later, she is the "pursued" Hero and acts as Dispatcher in sending her Helper Ninshubur to defend the *me* from Enki's Helpers. Her relationship to her Helper is an interesting one which should not be interpreted as "typical" passivity attributed to female characters in myth and tale: rescue from pursuit is a typical Helper "function," but in any case, the prominence of the Helper in acting to fulfill the Hero's quest is quite frequent in tale/myth plot structure (Propp: 79-83). It has also been suggested, however, that Ninshubur "represent(s) the inner spiritual resources of Inanna, which are intended for the greater good of Sumer" (Wolkstein and Kramer: 149). The myth ends with Inanna appearing as the new Donor of the *me* which she bestows upon Uruk.

3.32 A "Seeker-Hero" (one who sets out on a quest occasioned by a perceived "Lack") as opposed to a "Victim-Hero" (a hero who is driven out by an act of Villainy; see Propp: 36), Inanna fills with ease the typical action-roles usually ascribed to male characters in traditional compositions. Conversely, those "functions" typical for the narrative surface structure of fairy tales with a female as the main character (persecution in her father's house; seduction or other persecution in her husband's house; disguise as a male, etc.; see Dan for discussion) are not at all applicable to this text. At the same time, Inanna resists total "masculinization" and retains her feminine nature, not only in her celebration of her "wondrous vulva," but also in the text's repeated use of epithets such as "daughter" (dumu), "maiden" (ki-sikil, lú-ki-sikil), "woman" (munus), and "lady" (nin) (Farber-Flügge: 10-11). It is perhaps the representation of the goddess as a female character performing effectively in the male sphere of action which partially accounts for her acceptability to the patriarchal consciousness at a time when the nurturing goddesses fell from favor.

3.4 Of special interest is the context of the banquet scene, complete with overindulgence in intoxicants, as the occasion for the transfer of the much-coveted *me*. Jacobsen insists, with reference to this text and the other where Enki assigns left-over offices to Inanna after he has ordered the cosmos, that

> there is no contest of wits, Inanna wins by taking advantage of a moment when Enki's guard is down or when he wants to avoid trouble. Inanna understands her own limitations and her grandfather's superior ingenuity very well . . . (1976:114-15).

In fact, what we may be dealing with here is a "traditional episode" or "type-scene," in which a storyteller draws upon a number of conventional motifs which frequently occur together in order to advance the plot (Gottwald: 157-58, 217-19). Banquets do indeed appear in three other "divine journey" compositions where they are related to motifs of hospitality and sought-for blessing (Ferrara: 28, n. 21). We might term the particular type-scene found here the "banquet-contest" and note that the intoxication of one of the participants allows for the transference and redistribution of powers which might not otherwise take place. Enki seems to be a particularly frequent character in such episodes: in the myth "Enki and Ninmah" the existence of deformed or anomalous human beings is attributed to a drunken contest between Ninmah (= Ninhursag, the dethroned mother-goddess of the earth, "Ki") and Enki. Each being created by Ninmah is given a place and role in society by Enki, but the creature created by Enki is so deformed that Ninmah curses the god for his ineptitude, a charge which he seems to accept (Jacobsen, 1976:113-14). In "Enki's Journey to Nippur," he sets out a banquet in "the shrine Nippur" for Enlil, the god from whom Enki hopes to obtain blessing, and An, and we are told that "Enlil was made happy" (Ferrara: 148).

3.5 Another interpretation of Inanna's swift and decisive action in taking advantage of Enki's generosity when his heart was happy with drink may be put forward. Perusal of hierarchically ordered lists of high-ranking deities of the Sumerian pantheon shows a consistent tendency to demote the primal goddesses listed in favor of their male counterparts. This may be seen in the case of Nammu, the primal sea from whom the universe and gods are born. Her powers are given to Enki, and she seldom appears in godlists. Similarly, Ki (Mother) "Earth," Nammu's daughter, is first given third place, then fourth place in the godlists, following An ("Heaven"), Enlil ("Lord Air"), and Enki, and she is then called by the more general epithet, Ninhursag, "Queen of the Mountain." Kramer suggests that this is the work of "male theologians who manipulated the order of the divinities in accordance with what may well have been their chauvinistic predilections" (1974:14). Given the progressive decline of the status of women during the same periods, it is not difficult to see Inanna's deceptive and self-serving behavior as a reflection of the increasingly marginalized position of goddesses and women. Ranked only seventh in the divine hierarchy, Inanna must take quick advantage of any opportunities presented her— she does not become Queen of Heaven and Earth or Lady of Myriad Offices simply through her sexuality, but by the display of craft and courage as well. If she and the harlots she protects appear grasping and self-absorbed, this is a reflection of the constraints placed on female exercise of power in the societies in question. As "unladylike" as her behavior may appear to various commentators, in our myth she is envisioned as acting in the best of causes, to secure the well-being of her city and assure its continuing place among the city-states of Sumer. Lesser in status and prerogatives than her male antagonist she may be at the outset, but by the narrative's end, she has truly become Uruk's Queen of the *Me*, of equal, if not superior status to Enki, the foolish Lord of Wisdom.

3.6 Indirect parallels to the type-scene which allows Inanna's successful completion of her quest may be adduced in the Hebrew Bible. The wedding-feast prepared by Samson for his Philistine bride and her companions carries the overtone of "contest" in the riddling activity which aims at sublimation of aggressive male energies (Judg 14:10-20). The exchange of clothing for the successful solution of Samson's riddle clearly indicates a redistribution of power in the form of personal wealth (vv. 12-13), and the text contains reference to repetitive action (vv. 15, 17-18). The daughters of Lot use the stratagem of intoxicating their father to achieve their aims (Gen 19:30-38), again with the goal of enhancing the status of the childless women through the redistribution of (sexual) power residing in their father. Likewise, the redistribution of power which takes place on the threshing floor of Ruth 3 occurs when Boaz' heart is merry with drink, and includes sexual allusions as well. The banquet given by King Ahasuerus in Esther 1 may contain similar sexual overtones, perhaps accounting for Queen Vashti's unwillingness to attend her king and his servants. Later, the banquets prepared by Esther for Ahasuerus and Haman (Esth 5:4-8; 7:1-10) are in reality contests between Haman and Esther, and accomplish a successful reallocation of power from Haman to the Jews, with sexual implications once again present (7:7-8).

3.61 Judith 12-13 presents a fully developed banquet-contest typescene as the setting for the beautiful Judean's trickery. Here the "divine journey" of the seeker-goddess has become the quest of a human widow; both take place on behalf of their peoples. Holofernes' eunuch parallels the role of Isimud in greeting and inviting Judith into the feast (12:10-14); Judith's unnamed maid plays the role of "Helper" as Ninshubur does for Inanna (12:19; 13:3, 9-10). Emphasis on Judith's extreme beauty is reminiscent of Inanna's self-glorification of her femaleness at the outset of her quest. Like the banquet of Inanna and Enki, this one is prepared by the male of superior status, but the female of inferior status triumphs by keeping her head through the long hours of intoxicating indulgence. Empowered by her faith in the god of her fathers, Judith makes full use of her opponent's drunkenness. The fruit of her labors is given to benefit her city, and greeted with much rejoicing (13:4-14:5), as was Inanna's return to Uruk with the *me*.

4.0 From fourteenth century Anatolia we meet another deceptive goddess at a banquet in the Hattic Inaraš, a key player in "The Myth of Illuyankaš." This Hittite text, recorded by one Kellaš, a priest of Nerik, an important cultic center in the north of the Hittite kingdom, contains two versions of the aetiology of the *purulli* festival. Both are variants on the classic "Slaying the Dragon" motif, and it is likely that the composition was read at the high point of the festival as the battle was enacted (Gaster: 317). The *purulli* festival (probably meaning "of the earth") was celebrated in the spring of the year when the rivers, symbolized by dragons, were in danger of overflowing with the run-off from mountain snows (Gaster: 323), or in another modern interpretation, at the critical moment when drought—the dragon—must be conquered in order to insure the much-needed rains (Güterbock: 174). The festival, like so many Hittite practices and texts, appears to have a Hattic substratum, and judging by its length, was clearly one of the most important rituals performed (Gurney, 1958:106-7). Perhaps owing to its long history, the *purulli* myth seems to be particularly overlaid with folkloric "tale" elements, for generally, the "dragon" in ancient Near Eastern myth is a somber, frightening, and chaotic figure. The gluttonous, credulous Illuyankaš-dragon of the *purulli* myths is drawn much more along the lines of the ogres and giants who are invariably the simpleton foils of the tale hero (Gaster: 328-29). This is not to be wondered at since Güterbock has observed that Anatolian texts of Hattic origin show clear signs of having been "recently oral" compositions which were written down for their connection with rituals rather than as literary compositions (143).

4.1 The goddess Inaraš fills the critical role of Helper to the Weather-god in the *purulli* drama. One of the ^{d}KAL goddesses, she is thought by some to have been an autonomous Hattic goddess of great antiquity. In the Old Hittite period Inaraš has a temple of her own, whose cult language is Hattic, rather than Hittite (našili). In later times we meet her as the protective "genius" of the capital Ḫattušaš, as "Lord of the Oath," and the daughter of the Weather-god (Kammenhuber; Gurney, 1976:8-9). It is worth noting that there appear to be both a male and a female Inaraš, with the male being used interchangeably in the later periods. The figure in our text is the female Inaraš, as is seen by her liaison with her human Helper.

4.2 An outline of the action in the text runs as follows: after an initial defeat at the hands of the Illuyankaš-dragon at Kiškilušša, the Weather-god calls on the pantheon for assistance. In response, the goddess Inaraš prepares a feast along extremely generous lines, filling barrels to the brim with beer and wines. Going to the city of Ziguratta, she meets a mortal, one Hupašiyaš, whom she asks to help her. He agrees on condition that she have intercourse with him, which she does. Returning, she hides Hupašiyaš, adorns herself, and proceeds to lure the Illuyankaš-dragon and his cohorts (children?) from his lair. The Illuyankaš-dragons become sated and overcome with drink, to the point that they are unable to regain their burrow, whereupon Hupašiyaš springs out and binds them with a rope. The advance work being accomplished, the Weather-god enters and slays the dragon(s), while the pantheon looks on. The end of this first aetiology deals with the fate of Inaraš' human Helper. The goddess builds a house on a rock in Tarukka (also in the north) where she places Hupašiyaš, cautioning him not to look out of the window in her absence, lest he see his wife and children. On the twentieth day of her journey, the mortal of course violates this "Interdiction," and naturally happens to see his wife and children. The text is damaged at this point, but apparently Inaraš discovers Hupašiyaš' actions upon her return, as he implores her to be allowed to return home. She warns him once again not to open the window, and finally slays the faithless human, and the Weather-god sows weeds over the ill-fated house. Returning the Kiškilušša, Inaraš places her house in the hand of the king, so that "From the time on that we celebrated the first *Purulli* Festival, the hand of (the king has been supreme) in the . . . of Inaraš" (Goetze: 125-26; Gaster: 326-29).

4.3 A number of features are of interest here. First, as in so many cases "in Hattian myth, . . . the prime mover seems always to be a goddess" (Macqueen: 177), reflecting, no doubt, the high status enjoyed by Hattic goddesses in Anatolia before the influx of the Indo-european Hittites with their male Weather-gods. While Inanna was able to enjoy the role of Hero, the politics of invasion have reduced Inaraš to the role of Helper to the male Hero. Nevertheless, Inaraš is a particularly active Helper, performing a variety of helping functions, often with deadly effect (for Hupašiyaš and the Illuyankaš-dragon).

4.4 As in the texts concerning Inanna and the biblical women discussed above, sexuality plays a role in this type-scene. This motif occurs here in an especially critical way, for the "Donor Test" posed for Inaraš if she wishes to receive her Helper, and hence, accomplish her task, is that of sexual exchange. We may think of Tamar in Gen 38, who is also required to exchange her favors in order to receive the grudging Helper-Donor in the form of her father-in-law Judah, and the sexual connotations implicit in Ruth's acquisition of Boaz as Helper. Texts within and without Israel implicitly and explicitly condemn women and goddesses when they attempt to initiate sexual exchange ("El, Ashertu and the Storm-god," "Tale of Two Brothers," Gilgamesh Epic, Gen 39, Prov 7); episodes such as the one here where the male does the "propositioning" pass without moral comment, and are generally consummated successfully and without incident (cf. the interchange between Isis and Seth in "The Contendings of Horus and Seth," Simpson: 115). Apparently, negative moral evaluations of sexual exchange are more apt to be made when the gender of the one saying "Come! Lie with me!" is female, though 2 Sam 12-13 and the "Inanna and Shukalletuda" myth are welcome exceptions to the observation. Inanna acts with dispatch to avenge the wrong done her when she is raped by Shukalletuda, though it is not clear from the broken text whether or not she is successful, and one might argue also that this text views Inanna's reprisals as more horrendous than the deed which occasioned them.

4.41 The Hebrew Bible departs from its more customary lack of moral comment on the sexual exploitation of women in chastising David for his affair with Bathsheba, and condemning Tamar's assailant to death by her brother's (not her father's!) hand. Nevertheless, both of these biblical episodes could be understood as showing more concern for the "property rights" of the males whose females are illicitly taken. Further, in the case of Absalom and Tamar, the sexual exchange between Tamar and Amnon serves as the episode of Villainy whose subsequent ramifications drive Absalom out of his father's favor, showing that this is the narrative's true interest. Attention given to the fate of Tamar is minimal. Put another way, episodes of sexual exchange are more apt to be viewed as "routine" Donor Tests for the female protagonists of ancient Near Eastern texts, but the same situation fills the function of "Villainy" which drives the young hero out into adventure when the protagonist is male and the "seducer" female. The critical effects of the gender of characters on the narrative structure found in traditional compositions and their derivative literary genres could not be more clear, and any interpretive method which does not take such "sex differences" into consideration must be considered incomplete and probably misleading. In addition, since ancient texts by women are few and far between, field studies of modern traditional storytelling should be carefully examined for effects of the gender of the storyteller on narrative structure.

4.5 Unlike the Sumerian text above and the banquet-contest in Judith, in the Illuyankaš myth the giver of the feast, and not the guest(s), is the recipient of the redistributed power. This suggests that banquet typescenes might be further differentiated on the basis of who receives power. The episode under discussion is not so much a banquet "contest" where the guest has some hope of triumphing over the host, as it is a banquet "set-up" where the host premeditatedly violates rules of hospitality to the guest's detriment. The deceptive goddess seems to be equally at home in either literary setting, and whether she acts as guest or host, her deception is a critical aspect of the action. The banquet-contest occurs as the host's *response* to the arrival of the guest, and works to the guest's advantage. The banquet-"set-up" gives the advantage to the host, for it is not the natural, hospitable response to a guest, but a *trap* which has been crafted to resemble a positive or neutral occasion where the guest is lured into a false sense of security. Hence, some banquet type-scenes may fill the structural function of "Donor Tests" (Inanna), while others embody the function of "Struggle" where Heroes and Villains engage in direct conflict (Inaraš), with the former falling somewhere near the beginning of the narrative (or episode) and the latter type occuring near the end. One could also envision such a type-scene as the occasion for the unmasking of the False Hero, or False Bride, though this variation is not represented in any of the texts discussed here.

4.6 Given the violent end of the dragons, one cannot help being reminded of the fate of Sisera as he attends an impromptu "banquet" in the tent of Jael (Judg 5), and the dire warnings of death that attend the acceptance of an invitation to dine with Dame Folly in the form of her human alter ego, the loose woman with honeyed words (Prov 9:13-18). The message of these texts to their male audiences is clear: the very female who provides food, drink, shelter, and sexual services may turn out to be the vehicle of death, so beware! The ambivalent nature of the feminine is everywhere rehearsed in ancient Near Eastern narrative, whether the characters so maligned are human or divine. Further, such patriarchal ideology knows no boundaries of genre, and may be observed in myth (the texts discussed above), tale (see the treatment accorded to Job's unnamed but theologically astute wife), and saga (deceptive females in Genesis and elsewhere) alike.

4.61 To be sure, banquets and occasions of drinking generally carry negative connotations in the Hebrew Bible, regardless of whether they are "contest" or "set-up," or include women as guests or hosts, or not. This is the case precisely because power may be more easily wrested from the over-indulgent male who lets down his guard. The relaxing of inhibitions associated with the motifs of banquet/feast and drinking often leads to disaster or near-disaster: Noah's drunkenness prompts him to nakedness—the uncovering of power—and results in a curse on his overly eager son (Gen 9); the people of Israel are indulging themselves during the Golden Calf episode (Exod 32:6); Elah of Israel is killed by Zimri while drunk (1 Kgs 16); Job's children are feasting together when they are wiped out according to divine plan (Job 1:4,13); the banquets and drinking bouts given by Ben-Hadad (1 Kgs 20) and

Nabal (1 Sam 25) are signs of vainglorious behavior, and we are not surprised when disaster strikes down these characters subsequently. David's "set-up" banquet for Uriah the Hittite ends with that faithful retainer's death, though ironically, this is caused by Uriah's *refusal* of sexual exchange rather than by his indulgence (i.e., it is a "failed Donor Test"; 2 Sam 11). Absalom's banquet in 2 Sam 13 is the perfect "set-up" for revenge on his sister's rapist, conforming to the basic pattern found in the Illuyankaš myth, with sexual exchange (rape is its most violent form, since it is "robbery" rather than true exchange) taking place prior to the set-up. Given this strong narrative picture, no wonder sages warned against drunkenness so assiduously and prophets used such imagery effectively to evoke the redistribution of power that the Wrath of God would accomplish (Prov 20:1; 21:17; 23:20; 23:31; Isa 28:7; 49:26; 63:6; Jer 13:12-14; 25:15-29; 51:7, 39-40, 57; etc.)! It is left to Wisdom personified as woman and Yhwh to reverse this trend of the banquet which leads to disaster: the feasts set by these two in Prov 9 and Isa 25:6-9 lead to life, insight, the swallowing up of death, and the end of reproach.

5.0 Our discussion of the goddess-deceiver at the banquet, playing the roles of both guest (Inanna) and host (Inaraš), does not exhaust the literary motif of the deceptive goddess in ancient Near Eastern literature. The figure of Isis most especially deserves attention in this regard. Her trickery of Re on behalf of future sufferers from snake-bite in "The God and His Unknown Name of Power" (Pritchard: 12-14) and her shape-changing deceptions of Seth in "The Contendings of Horus and Seth" show the goddess-deceiver in action outside of "food service" contexts.

5.1 What is of interest both in Isis' deceptions and those discussed above is their pragmatic effectiveness: the goddesses' deception is never mere whim, or worse, moral defect, but action suited to the requirements of the situation at hand and the structural needs of the narrative. Deception, as practiced by the divine females of the ancient Near East, must also be judged by the overall outcome of the action: she deceives, not on her own behalf, but on behalf of city, high-god, or in Isis' case, on behalf of humankind in general or her son Horus. These observations conform very well to the patterns noted in studies of the male or animal Tricksters of Native American and West African mythology. There we find these mediating figures acting in disruptive, ambivalent ways even as they integrate the sacred and profane worlds. Motifs of excess in sexuality and appetite, common to Trickster mythology (Radin: 136), also appear in our myths, though transmuted to fit both the genre and gender of the texts at hand.

5.2   Still, the mediating function of the actions of the deceptive goddess is related not only to the nature of the Trickster figures themselves but also to the agendas of mythographers and theologians. The goddess who acts on her own behalf rather than for others is too frightening a figure to appear with any frequency in myth or cult. The ambivalent and terrifying figure of the powerful divine female is domesticated into the Helper of the gods and Donor to the city-state. In this fashion, patriarchy finds a literary method for absorbing female power and making it acceptable (i.e., subservient) to the dominant ideology. Both Inanna and Inaraš may act with autonomy and dispatch, but Enki and the Weather-god are presented as the true sources of power or will-to-act, upon whom the goddesses' actions are to some extent dependent. By aiding the gods in their struggles against the chaos wrought by drought (Inaraš), destructive divine forces (Isis), or seeking the god as a source of power for her own city (Inanna), the goddess in fact aids the human communities who look to the cult of the gods for protection. In myth, the deceiver paradoxically becomes Helper and Donor by means of her deception, and humanity profits from the redistribution of power thereby accomplished.[4]

WORKS CONSULTED

Dan, Ilana
    1977   "The Innocent Persecuted Heroine: An Attempt at a Model for the Surface Level of the Narrative Structure of the Female Fairy Tale." Pp. 13-30 in *Patterns in Oral Literature*. Ed. Heda Jason and D. Segal. The Hague: Mouton.

Dundes, Alan, ed.
    1984   *Sacred Narrative: Readings in the Theory of Myth*. Berkeley: University of California.

Farber-Flügge, Gertrud
    1973   *Der Mythos "Inanna and Enki" unter besonderer Berücksichtigung der Liste der me*. Studie Pohl, 10. Rome: Biblical Institute Press.

Ferrara, A. J.
    1973   *Nanna-Suen's Journey to Nippur*. Studia Pohl, Series Major, 2. Rome: Biblical Institute Press.

---

[4] My thanks to my students Lisa Schoenwetter, Imogene Stulken, and Pat Sodano for interesting me in the goddess literature discussed here, and to Claudia Camp, David Jobling, and J. Cheryl Exum for encouraging me to write on this topic. Special thanks go to Lois Happe, Tim Norheim, and Mary DeSocio for their technical assistance in the preparation of this manuscript, and to my husband Helper, Craig Fontaine, for his assistance in dealing with software-trauma.

Fuchs, Esther
    1985   "Who is Hiding the Truth? Deceptive Women and Biblical Androcentrism." Pp. 137-44 in *Feminist Perspectives on Biblical Scholarship*. Ed. Adela Yarbro Collins. Chico, CA: Scholars Press.

Gaster, Theodor H.
    1950   *Thespis: Ritual, Myth and Drama in the Ancient Near East*. New York: Henry Schuman.

Goetze, Albrecht
    1969   "The Myth of Illuyankaš." Pp. 125-26 in Pritchard, ed.

Gottwald, Norman K.
    1985   *The Hebrew Bible: A Socio-Literary Introduction*. Philadelphia: Fortress Press.

Grahn, Judy
    1982   "From Sacred Blood to the Curse and Beyond." Pp. 265-79 in *The Politics of Women's Spirituality*. Ed. Charlene Spretnak. Garden City, N.Y.: Anchor Press.

Güterbock, H. G.
    1961   "Hittite Mythology." Pp. 139-79 in *Mythologies of the Ancient World*. Ed. with an Introduction by Samuel N. Kramer. Garden City, N.Y.: Doubleday-Anchor.

Gurney, O. R.
    1952   *The Hittites*. England: Penguin Books.
    1958   "Hittite Kingship." Pp. 105-21 in *Myth, Ritual, and Kingship*. Ed. S. H. Hooke. Oxford, U.K.: Oxford University Press.
    1976   *Some Aspects of Hittite Religion*. Oxford, U.K.: Oxford University Press.

Haas, V.
    1970   *Der Kult von Nerik: Ein Beitrag zur hethitischen Religionsgeschichte*. Studia Pohl, 4. Rome: Pontifical Institute.

Hallo, William W. and Van Dijk, J. J. A.
    1968   *The Exaltation of Inanna*. New Haven: Yale University Press.

Hoffner, H. A.
    1968   "Birth and Name-giving in Hittite texts." *JNES* 27:198-203.

Jacobsen, Thorkild
    1970   *Toward the Image of Tammuz and Other Essays on Mesopotamian History and Culture*. Ed. William L. Moran. Harvard Semitic Series, XXI. Cambridge: Harvard University Press.
    1976   *The Treasures of Darkness: A History of Mesopotamian Religion*. New Haven: Yale University Press.

Kammenhuber, A.
                "Inar." *Reallexikon der Assyriologie*, V:89-90.

Kramer, Samuel Noah
- 1952 *Enmerkar and the Lord of Aratta: A Sumerian Epic Tale of Iraq and Iran.* Museum Monographs. Philadelphia: University of Pennsylvania Museum.
- 1956 *From the Tablets of Sumer.* Indian Hills, CO: Falcon's Wing Press.
- 1963 *The Sumerians: Their History, Culture and Character.* Chicago: University of Chicago Press.
- 1972 *Sumerian Mythology: A Study of Spiritual and Literary Achievement in the Third Millennium B.C.*, rev. ed. Philadelphia: University of Pennsylvania Press.
- 1974 "Poets and Psalmists, Goddesses and Theologians: Literary, Religious, and Anthropological Aspects of the Legacy of Sumer." *Monographs on the Ancient Near East* 1:3-21.

Lamphere, Louise
- 1974 "Strategies, Cooperation, and Conflict Among Women in Domestic Groups." Pp. 97-112 in *Woman, Culture, and Society.* Ed. Michelle Z. Rosaldo and Louise Lamphere. Stanford: Stanford University Press.

Lévi-Strauss, Claude
- 1963 "The Structural Study of Myth." Pp. 206-31 in *Structural Anthropology.* Trans. Claire Jacobson and Brooke G. Schoepf. New York: Basic Books.

Macqueen, J. G.
- 1975 "Hattian Mythology and Hittite Monarchy." *Anatolian Studies* 9:171-88.

Ochshorn, Judith
- 1985 "Ishtar and Her Cult." Pp. 16-28 in *The Book of the Goddess, Past and Present.* Ed. Carl Olson. New York: Crossroad.

Pritchard, James B., ed.
- 1969 *Ancient Near Eastern Texts Relating to the Old Testament*, 3rd ed. with Supplement. Princeton: Princeton University Press.

Propp, Vladimir
- 1968 *Morphology of the Folktale*, 2nd ed., rev. Trans. Laurence Scott. Austin: University of Texas Press.

Radin, Paul
- 1956 *The Trickster: A Study in American Indian Mythology.* New York: Greenwood.

Reid, Susan
- 1974 "Myth as Metastructure of the Fairÿtale." Pp. 151-72 in *Soviet Structural Folkloristics: Texts by Meletinsky, Nekludov, Novik and Seqal with Tests of the Approach by Jilek and Jilek-Aall,*

Reid and Layton. Vol. I. Ed. Pierre Maranda. Approaches to Semiotics, 43. The Hague: Mouton.

Sasson, Jack M.
1979 *Ruth: A New Translation with a Philological Commentary and a Formalist-Folklorist Interpretation.* Baltimore: Johns Hopkins University Press.

Simpson, William K., ed.
1973 *The Literature of Ancient Egypt: An Anthology of Stories, Instructions, and Poetry.* New Haven: Yale University Press.

Taylor, J. Glen
1982 "The Song of Deborah and Two Canaanite Goddesses." *JSOT* 23:99-108.

Wakeman, Mary K.
1981 "Feminist Revision of the Matriarchal Hypothesis." *Anima* 7:83-96.

Wolkstein, Diane and Kramer, Samuel Noah
1983 *Inanna, Queen of Heaven and Earth: Her Stories and Hymns from Sumer.* New York: Harper & Row.

INTERROGATING BIBLICAL DECEPTION AND TRICKSTER THEORIES: NARRATIVES OF PATRIARCHY OR POSSIBILITY?

Kathleen M. Ashley
University of Southern Maine

In their examination of female deception in biblical narratives, the foregoing essays have drawn repeatedly upon theories of the trickster, explanatory models of trickery based on studies of Native American, South American, West African, and European folklore and mythology. The various trickster theories are deployed together as interpretive tools, or if one among them is chosen its choice is rarely justified explicitly; yet the available theories represent widely disparate models of symbolic activity. They thus offer divergent, even contradictory, explanations of how trickster figures work within their tales as well as differing views of the social uses of trickster stories.

My response to the five essays on female deception will trace a double path. First, analysis of the various theories of the trickster will be used to clarify the arguments made about biblical deceivers. Then, these essays—all of which draw upon emerging feminist methodologies to raise the issue of gender's effect upon the construction and reception of narratives—will be used to interrogate trickster theory, which has not yet confronted the issue of gender.

Sociological theory

Perhaps the most straightforward of the theories of trickster behavior might be called the "sociological." It forms the basis of Naomi Steinberg's analysis of Israelite tricksters. As she says, "evidence from the social sciences suggests that individuals resort to the use of trickery under certain social conditions. In particular, when individuals lack authority—whether it be political, economic, religious, or domestic authority—they resort to strategies which allow them to achieve their goals and gain compliance with their wishes. I understand trickery to be a kind of power available to persons in a subordinate position . . ." (3.1).

The trickster tales which most compellingly bear out this thesis are those of Afro-America. Research has shown that the West African divine trickster, such as the Legba of Dahomy or the Eshu of Yoruba, did not survive transplantation to the United States, or their traits were transferred to the Judaeo-Christian devil (Genovese: 218-219). Animal tricksters did remain popular, however, and Lawrence Levine points out that in both African and Afro-American tales the primary trickster figures were "weak, relatively powerless creatures who attain their ends through the application of native wit and guile rather than power or authority: the Hare or Rabbit in East Africa, Angola, and parts of Nigeria; the Tortoise among the Yoruba, Ibo, and Edo peoples of Nigeria; the Spider throughout much of West Africa including Ghana, Liberia, and Sierra Leone; Brer Rabbit in the United States" (99). He goes on to note that the African animal tricksters were "obsessed with manipulating the strong and reversing the normal structure of power and prestige" (101), and that the slave, trapped within an even more rigid authority system, found these trickster tales ideally suited to wage symbolic assault upon the powerful.

As coded tales of social protest, whose powerless tellers could identify with the imperative of trickery, Afro-American trickster stories lend themselves without strain to a sociological analysis. Steinberg would extend this type of analysis to biblical narratives of lying and deception. The partial list of tricksters in the Hebrew Bible she gives in §4.1 include both men and women whose strategies of trickery spring from a position of social disadvantage. She makes the significant point that, given the patriarchal culture reflected in the Bible, it is not surprising that more women than men are forced to resort to deceit in order to influence events; however, such deceit comes from their position of powerlessness in the society, not from some essential female nature which is inherently deceptive (4.4).

The problem with a straightforward sociological analysis comes when the tellers of trickster tales are no longer the powerless but the power brokers themselves. The Hebrew tales of deception occur within narratives constructed primarily by men in positions of moral and literary authority, although Steinberg comments on folkloric origins: "Presumably before the biblical literature was considered to be authoritative Scripture, at a time before it was contextualized as religious tradition, it, like other folklore, explicitly was recognized to refer to the sexual and the comical" (2.1). Steinberg confronts this fact by abandoning sociological theory to take up structuralist accounts of how myths and folktales function (5.3). Her allusions to the work of Beidelman, Edwards, and Lévi-Strauss are brief and not applied in detail to the biblical texts, but they raise the possibility that trickster tales could be used to comment on the social problem of order and disorder.

A purely sociological model of the trickster tends to be reductive: Brer Rabbit is the slave, the larger animals are the white masters, etc. The tricks of the underdog are laughable and legitimated by his weakness. But the weak alone are not characterized by trickery; those in power often resort to equally devious methods, so that stories like those of Brer Rabbit can be used to satirize the powerful and need not refer solely to the structurally powerless. Levine suggests that trickster tales offered a "prolonged and telling parody of white society" (121), while Barbara Babcock and Paul Radin have noted that the antics of the Winnebago trickster Wakdjunkaga are often explicitly satirical of tribal systems of rank, kinship, and morality (Babcock: 178; Radin: 151-53).

As a point of departure, the sociological theory of trickery works well for deceivers in the Hebrew Bible; however, its limitations require that it be supplemented by insights from other theories of the trickster.

Structuralist theory

The fundamental problem with a purely sociological analysis of the trickster is that of referent; which figure in the tale represents which social group is often difficult to determine, and the ambiguity is fatal to the theory. Structuralist theory, however, founds itself upon ambivalence and ambiguity. The anthropologist Edmund Leach has written that

> in every myth system we will find a persistent sequence of binary discriminations as between human/superhuman, mortal/immortal, male/female, legitimate/illegitimate, good/bad . . . followed by a "mediation" of the paired categories thus distinguished.
>
> "Mediation" (in this sense) is always achieved by introducing a third category which is "abnormal" or "anomalous" in terms of ordinary "rational" categories. Thus myths are full of fabulous monsters, incarnate gods, virgin mothers. This middle ground is abnormal, non-natural, holy. It is typically the focus of all taboo and ritual observance (320).

Mythical figures like tricksters bridge the original categories and are therefore inherently ambivalent and often morally ambiguous.

Carole Fontaine's essay posits female deceivers in both human and goddess form as the mediator figures in ancient Near Eastern mythology. "Whether the woman in question uses deception to achieve goals approved by patriarchy (Rebekah, Tamar, Ruth, Rahab, Jael, Judith) or is depicted as a deceiver whose actions threaten the patriarchal order (Jezebel, Potiphar's wife, Dame Folly), the strategy for effective action most closely associated with women characters in the Hebrew Bible is a morally ambivalent one" (1.0). Of the relations between the Hebrew text and its surrounding Near Eastern myths, Fontaine notes that "'goddess functions' (actions performed by godesses to advance the action in their stories) are often transferred to the Hebrew God, that god's human (male) surrogate-heroes, the people Israel, and less frequently to Israel's women" (2.1). The logic of structuralism asks us to see trickster functions as solutions to problems, and thus as morally neutral, somehow ouside the language of moral norms (or good and evil). The very capacity of mediators to be outside normal categories and to bridge them is what allows them to be creative, to represent new solutions, but that power is perceived as dangerous and therefore often taboo as Laura Makarius argues. Of tricksters and gods of myth, Lévi-Strauss argues that they are halfway between two polar terms and must therefore retain something of the duality, be contradictory—good and bad at the same time (226-227). Not surprisingly, they give rise to ambivalent responses, even when they are performing socially valuable deeds.

Fontaine's analysis is based primarily upon the syntagmatic structuralism of Propp rather than the paradigmatic structuralism of Leach and Lévi-Strauss. According to Fontaine, the Sumerian goddess Inanna performs the functions typical in Proppian plot structures of the male hero rather than the female protagonist (3.32). As a "type-scene," the banquet at which Inanna ouwits a drunken Enki is interpreted as a means by which powers are transferred and redistributed (3.4), although Fontaine also goes back to a sociological analysis when she says that "given the progressive decline of the status of women during the same periods, it is not difficult to see Inanna's deceptive and self-serving behavior as a reflection of the increasingly marginalized position of goddesses and women" (3.5). Perhaps most important is the fact that the redistribution of power which takes place through banquet drunkenness scenes—whether in Near Eastern goddess stories or in such stories of the Hebrew Bible as those of Samson, the daughters of Lot, Ruth, Esther, and Judith (3.6), Noah's and Job's children, Absalom, etc. (4.61)—tends to be for the benefit of the larger group. "In myth, the deceiver paradoxically becomes Helper and Donor by means of her deception, and humanity profits from the redistribution of power thereby accomplished" (5.2).

Structuralism, whether of the Proppian syntagmatic or Lévi-Straussian paradigmatic type, has little interest in returning its mythological logic to any particular social context. What local features indigenous to one society might affect the portrayal of the trickster and his/her tales, structuralism is not equipped to examine. For that we must go to cultural hermeneutics, which pays considerable attention to the cultural context in which specific stories are told.

Cultural Hermeneutics

Claudia Camp's essay refers explicitly to the cultural hermeneutics approach of Robert Pelton, whose study of West African trickster myths draws on concepts of Clifford Geertz and Victor Turner, among others. Camp says, "One may generalize about the trickster as a combination liar, buffoon, and culture-hero, but these traits are always narratively manifest in culturally specific ways that enable a given culture to interpret itself to itself" (0.3). As Pelton puts it, "The important point is not how many trickster features Ananse, for example, may possess, but how his structure works in relation to the other structures of Ashanti society and how it exists as a peculiarly Ashanti discovery of significance" (16).

As a hermeneutic for understanding the relationship between the Wisdom and Strange Woman figures of Proverbs 1-9, the paradigm of the trickster undercuts the surface message of "absolute opposition between good and evil as represented in these two figures" to suggest their paradoxical unity (6.1). Tricksters may represent both the forces of creation and destruction. Semiotically speaking, knowledge of evil is necessary for the knowledge of good, and societies constitute their own boundaries by defining what is "other." Susan Stewart notes that "as an embodiment of disparate domains, trickster is analogous to the process of metaphor, the incorporation of opposites into a new configuration. He represents both the breakdown and the emergence of the classifications constituting culture" (62). In language, specifically, the deceit, lying, and disorder associated with the trickster behavior of such figures as the Ashante's Ananse, the Fon's Legba, and the Yoruba's Eshu are generative of human discourse, not opposed to it. Thus Camp argues that at the heart of wisdom thought lies the trickster's paradox: death does yield life (2.31).

Camp sees the negative in Proverbs not so much as biological death but as separation from deity and community, especially notable in post-exilic literature which includes Proverbs. The dangerous Strange Woman is acknowledged as a danger *within* the community's boundaries, while Wisdom's boundary crossing is also striking. Both represent the "dangerously disordering process" through which life becomes available to Israel (2.4). The ambiguity of the female imagery also reflects "the moral ambiguity of the deity which stands in the shadows of Eden and bursts forth in the Joban whirlwind," Camp argues (4.42).

Camp draws finally on Victor Turner's concept of liminality, the "betwixt and between" state in rituals, to suggest the liminal as a source of personal and social regeneration. "Typically, in Israel, the source of power and love would have been Yhwh, usually imaged as male, mediated through the male power structures of society" (5.22). Women represented the antithesis of normal social and theological structures, in Turner's term they were "anti-structural." In Proverbs, however, the female becomes the source of the community's life, not in the usual biological sense of child-bearing but in the sociocultural and religious domains. The female imagery symbolized fundamental values shared by the community, serving as a "life-and-identity-source" in the post-exilic period when the male power structure, the monarchy, had vanished (5.23). Camp concludes that the "wisdom tradition" does seem to be set apart from "mainstream Yahwism," but "what the trickster paradigm makes clear is that Yahwism could not long exist without it" (5.3).

A very large body of cultural theory, ranging from Mary Douglas and Victor Turner to Mikhail Bakhtin, has suggested the power of the socially marginal to become symbolically and ritually central. Those who are not identified with powerful social structures often perform the service for the whole of reminding it of *communitas*, of fundamental human values which the social order violates in everyday practice. Since *communitas* is located outside the social hierarchy, its representatives in many cultures tend to be women, as Turner's discussion of rites of status reversal shows (183-85). In classic Greek drama—Aristophanes' *Lysistrata* and the plays of Euripides—salvation often comes from or through women, who represent Panhellenism and religious values which transcend the male world of the *polis* (Foley: 91). Insofar as females in biblical narrative are also social marginals, often morally ambiguous, or in violation of cultural categories, they may be available to the society as a means of renewal or change. They may use strategies which are not normally valid, including deception, or they may exploit linguistic ambiguity to redefine terms in order to provide a solution to problems.

Johanna Bos' essay on three stories of women who act in the interests of Israel, although very much in contradiction to female norms, takes this critical approach. Without citing cultural theorists, Bos arrives at their conclusions; the choice of Tamar, for example, is "not merely for the continuation of the patriarchal family embodied in the house of Judah, it is a choice for the building of a house which reflects God's choice for Israel and for the creation" (0.6). Bos explicitly bases her methodology on Alter's literary analysis (1.0), which however she inverts. In the place of his "type-scene" she discovers "counter-type-scenes" in Genesis 38, Judges 4:17-22, and Ruth, where the male protagonist fails in pursuit of fortune and a woman then moves to the center of the narrative to change the course of events (1.3). Bos concludes that "both patriarchy and counter-voice can be heard in the narrative of Tamar and her family." The patriarchal structures may not be changed, but Tamar's actions challenge the notion that "the promises of God are advanced through male initiative alone" (2.6.8). The story of Yael in Judges 4 and 5 is one of role reversal, with the powerful (males) showing weakness and the weak (females) showing strength. As Bos notes, women become the "helpers" through whom God accomplishes victory (3.6.9). The story of Ruth is even more anomalous, since it becomes not the romance of conventional reading but a powerful alliance between two women (4.4.4.3). The literary methodologies Bos uses yield valuable insights but do not provide a theoretical framework capable of accounting for the power given to women in these stories. Some form of cultural theory whose focus is symbolic action or representation appears to be necessary.

Moral Psychology and the Ideology of Genre

None of the essays in this volume makes systematic use of the original and influential theory of the trickster figure formulated by Paul Radin in his collection and study of Winnebago trickster tales. According to Radin, the trickster represents a primordial being, obsessed with hunger and sexuality, an archaic *speculum mentis* (xxiv). Drawing on Radin's theory, Jung argues that the undifferentiated consciousness represented in trickster myths holds an "earlier low intellectual and moral level before the eyes of the more highly developed individual" (Radin: 207), reminding him/her of the evolution of morality on which civilization rests.

Although the essay by Esther Fuchs does not depend upon any of the trickster theories described above, it does make the assumption also made by Radin that amoral or antisocial behaviors such as rapacious hunger, sexuality, or trickery carry ethical charge; they are evidence of a figure's lower moral status. Thus, Fuchs argues, by suppressing explanations of motivation, suspending authorial judgment, and avoiding closure in such stories of female deception as Rachel's (Gen 31:19-36), the biblical narrative allows for an association between femininity and deceptiveness. The implication of the story is that deception in women is not a problem requiring punishment or reformation, which Fuchs interprets as a denial and demeaning of female experience (1.1). She concludes that the "textual failure to problematize, challenge, and resolve the moral ambiguity attributed to female characters reflects an epistemological economy which predicates moral judgment on a character's sexual identity" (5.2).

The discussions of structuralist trickster theories and cultural hermeneutics have suggested that "moral ambiguity" may be an indicator of position within a transformational system. The ambiguities or paradoxes expressed through trickster figures make them "good to think with" for their cultures. In order to decide whether trickery, deception, or ambiguity are to be interpreted within the ethical categories of good and evil, we need to examine biblical genres and the larger issue of the ideology of genre.

The generic complexity of the Hebrew Bible has been alluded to in several of the essays. The trickster materials used by the scholars in this volume come primarily from folktale and traditional mythology, raising the additional issue of how such folklore material is related to the biblical texts (Steinberg 2.1; Camp 0.22; Fontaine 2.1). The biblical narrative, whose protagonists are for the most part recognizably human beings rather than tricky animals or shape-shifting gods, also makes it difficult to confront our own assumptions about characterization which are typically based on the novel genre. The application of ethical criteria to characters in biblical stories raises the question of whether such narratives share a focus on the individual subject with the nineteenth century novel.

Fredric Jameson's comments on genre in "Magical Narratives" are pertinent to our examination of the ideological implications of genres in biblical material. He notes that Lévi-Straussian paradigmatic structuralism succeeds in eliminating Proppian notions of the *actant* and of narrative diachrony because the narratives with which he was working (folklore, especially South American) are "preindividualistic";

> they emerge from a social world in which the psychological subject has not yet been constituted as such, and therefore in which later categories of the subject, such as "character," are not relevant. Hence the bewildering fluidity of these narrative strings, in which human subjects are ceaselessly transformed into animals or objects and back again; in which nothing like narrative "point of view," let alone "identification" or "empathy" with this or that protagonist emerges; in which not even the position of an individual storyteller or "sender" (*destinataire*) can be conceptualized without contradiction (124).

Jameson argues that Propp was projecting later categories of the individual subject anachronistically onto narrative forms which preceed the subject's emergence, "ideological categories that it was the secret purpose of later texts (for example, nineteenth century novels) to produce and project" (124).

Fuchs does confront the objection that biblical narration in general shows varying degrees of reticence or ambiguity in characterization; "narrative gapping and ambiguity are among the major literary hallmarks of the biblical text" (1.4). She argues, however, that suspension of authorial judgment is more pronounced with female characterizations, concluding that "the systematic differences in the biblical representation of deceptive men and women is crucial for our understanding of the interdependence of biblical poetics and the Bible's patriarchal ideology" (7.3). As someone whose expertise lies outside biblical scholarship, I am not in a position to dispute the details of this essay's analysis—nor is its conclusion necessarily in dispute—but the lack of theoretical scrutiny given to terms like "representation" or "characterization" is striking. All the essays in this volume refer repeatedly to "patriarchal ideology," again without defining the terms. If feminist criticism is not to be reductive, it must foster discourse of theoretical breadth and subtlety. It must also allow the space for exploration and speculation that this issue of *Semeia* clearly affords its contributors.

Interrogating Trickster Theories
Having used the various theories of the trickster to respond to the essays on biblical deception, we will now turn to some issues raised in the essays to challenge traditional trickster theories, and to confront the politics of interpretation.

In various ways, usually implicitly, the essays demand that attention be paid to reception by an audience or interpretive community as part of the interpretation of any story. Most theories of the trickster have assumed they were narratives recounted orally within a small traditional or tribal society. The "interpretive community" (to use Stanley Fish's phrase) is assumed to be unproblematic, to share the same interpretive horizons and therefore to be capable of receiving the same messages from a given story. Though folklorists and anthropologists are beginning to question such assumptions, even more pressing problems arise with regard to folklore and myths embedded within written texts which are then received by widely different interpretive communities, for example readers of the Hebrew Bible.

In a recent article, Daniel Cottom discusses the importance of contingencies which enter into the interpretation of a joke or any other kind of text. Cottom argues that

> there is no ideal political authority in *eloquentia*, institutions, communities of readers, or anywhere else but rather a complexly overdetermined conflict about authority, which cannot be adequately described as long as students in a classroom or members in an institution are isolated from the historical contingencies involved in differences of race, class, wealth, gender, and so on. The demand for the inclusion of such contingencies may seem crude within the protocols of literary theory, but its effect should be to restore to institutions the historical complexity that is erased from their every aspect when they are described as utopias of consensus. . . . The demand of theory should rather be to describe the relation between poetics and politics that is implicated in the very conception of the cultural institution within which the act of reading is seen as taking place (580).

Cottom concludes that, analyzed historically, "the meaning of a particular text is theoretically unlimited, since political perspectives are as various as imaginable subjectivities; and yet the range of meaning will be limited by the differences of power that a particular reading puts into play" (585).

All the essays in this volume demand that the contingency of gender be taken seriously. Feminist theory in general has paid inadequate attention to the contingencies of class and ethnicity, but theories of the trickster (whether psycho-social, structural, or cultural) have not addressed the issue of gender. Several of these essays suggest that female characters may be "marked" differently than male characters, even when performing similar actions. Is Inanna's "wondrous vulva" (Wolstein and Kramer: 12) truly analogous to Trickster's gigantic, errant penis (Radin:18-19)? Is a female boundary-crosser more negatively inflected than a male breaker of norms? Where females are not negatively marked for behaving in ways like (or different from) males, what significance accrues to the portrayal of such actions within texts or genres written by and for men? Is the meaning different than it would be if the text were produced by women within a "non-patriarchal" culture? What about reception by females rather than males? Several essays have cited male critics whose interpretations conflict with those of feminist critics. From the construction of the text to its reception, every stage contains the potential for gender to have political significance.

A project like this one also exemplifies the difficulty of feminist analysis on complex and cross-cultural texts. Not only are feminist methodologies in an emergent state, but gender itself is a "cultural construction"; it "means" different things within different cultures. Gender distinctions, references to sexual functions, sexual pollution, all may be used as symbolic language for the relations between parts of society rather than necessarily expressing the actual relations between the sexes, as Mary Douglas points out in her study of *Purity and Danger* (3-4).

Clearly, as all these essays imply, a high priority within future feminist scholarship must be assigned to the task of specifying the interpretive context for any text. The political significance of a story, whether we are speaking of trickster tales or biblical narratives, cannot be determined outside of its interpretive context.

In this regard, Janice Radway's study of contemporary popular literature, *Reading the Romance*, is pertinent. Her conclusion takes up the thorny issue of whether the genre of women's romance fiction should be considered fundamentally conservative or incipiently oppositional (209-22), the same question that studies of female deception in biblical narrative might raise. On the one hand, Radway points out that ethnographic study of actual romance readers shows how the activity addresses needs for independence and emotional nurturance not met by patriarchal institutions, and symbolically validates female ideals of love and personal interaction over male values of competition and public achievement. In doing so, the genre can act as a collective female ritual to explore the consequences of women's social condition and offer a potential basis for protest and change. On the other hand, as Radway also notes, the reading of romance appears to disarm the woman's impulse for real social change—for challenging the system of marital relations in which women are relegated to a totally private world of home and family—by naturalizing and mystifying the very conditions which gave rise to the need for romance. The romance thus "avoids questioning the institutionalized basis of patriarchal control over women even as it serves as locus of protest against some of its emotional consequences" (217).

The solution to the dilemma of ideological complexity may be, as Radway suggests, to distinguish analytically between meanings inscribed within the text and those that emerge from the act of reading a text. The analytic distinction "then empowers us to question whether the significance of the act of reading itself might, under some conditions, contradict, undercut, or qualify the significance of producing a particular kind of story" (210). Compared with a Harlequin novel, biblical narrative is likely to have even more potential for "oppositional" readings—given the complexity of its production and the contradictory codes inscribed in it. Just as Radway sees the women readers of romance novels using the act of reading against the confining structures of middle-class marriage, as an implicit critique of those social arrangements, so folklorists have interpreted trickster tales as challenging the categories and structures by which people have chosen to live. As norm-breakers, boundary-crossers, paradoxical beings, tricksters embody other ways of doing things. Barre Toelken's research on Navaho Coyote tales elicited the response that "Through the stories everything is made possible" (155). Yellowman, the teller of tales, thus "sees Coyote less as a trickster per se and more as an enabler whose actions, good or bad, bring certain ideas and actions into the field of possibility, a model who symbolizes abstractions in terms of real entities" (155-56). Tricksters make available for thought the way things are not but might be; their stories can function as critiques of the *status quo* as well as models for other possible arrangements. Whether and how such stories activate those functions depends upon the interpretive community in which they are told.

No doubt such stories can and have been used to reinforce the *status quo* which they appear to oppose. The issues in this debate over deception in biblical women echo those of commentators on carnival. "Carnivalesque" behaviors like role reversal seem to act out protest against the politically powerful, while at the same time consolidating the established order. Peter Stallybrass and Allon White, writing on *The Politics and Poetics of Transgression*, note that to argue the issue of whether carnivals are intrinsically radical or conservative is to essentialize the form. "The most that can be said in the abstract is that for long periods carnival may be a stable and cyclical ritual with no noticeable politically transformative effects but that, given the presence of sharpened political antagonism, it may often act as a *catalyst* and *site of actual and symbolic struggle*" (14). Transgressive forms like carnival and transgressive images like deceptive women take on political power by being used or interpreted in concrete historical contexts. Whether that power supports the "patriarchy" or gives rise to new possibilities depends upon the interpreter and the historical situation. The essays in this issue of *Semeia* as they interrogate traditional biblical scholarship and explore a variety of interpretive contexts for female deception open up the biblical narratives to new possibilities.

WORKS CONSULTED

Babcock, Barbara
    1975   "'A Tolerated Margin of Mess': The Trickster and His Tales Reconsidered." *Journal of the Folklore Institute* 11: 147-86.

Bakhtin, Mikhail
    1984   *Rabelais and His World*. Trans. Hélène Iswolsky. Bloomington: Indiana University Press.

Cottom, Daniel
    1985   "The Enchantment of Interpretation." *Critical Inquiry* 11:573-94.

Douglas, Mary
    1966   *Purity and Danger: An Analysis of Concepts of Pollution and Taboo*. New York: Praeger.

Edwards, Jay
    1984   "Structural Analysis of the Afro-American trickster tale." Pp. 81-103 in *Black Literature and Literary Theory*. Ed. Henry Louis Gates, Jr. New York: Methuen.

Fish, Stanley
    1980   *Is There a Text in This Class? The Authority of Interpretive Communities*. Cambridge: Harvard.

Foley, Helene
    1985   *Ritual Irony: Poetry and Sacrifice in Euripides*. Ithaca: Cornell.

Geertz, Clifford
    1973   *The Interpretation of Cultures*. New York: Basic Books.

Genovese, Eugene
    1974   *Roll, Jordan, Roll: The World the Slaves Made.* New York: Pantheon.

Jameson, Fredric
    1981   *The Political Unconscious: Narrative as a Socially Symbolic Act.* Ithaca: Cornell.

Jung, C. G.
    1972   "On the Psychology of the Trickster Figure." Pp. 195-211 in *The Trickster.* Ed. Paul Radin. New York: Schocken.

Leach, Edmund
    1973   "Genesis as Myth." Pp. 317-29 in *European Literary Theory and Practice.* Ed. Vernon W. Gras. New York: Dell.

Levine, Lawrence W.
    1974   "'Some Go Up and Some Go Down': The Meaning of the Slave Trickster." Pp. 94-124 in *The Hofstadter Aegis: A Memorial.* Ed. Stanley Elkins and Eric McKitrick. New York: Knopf.

Lévi-Strauss, Claude
    1963   "The Structural Study of Myth." Pp. 206-31 in *Structural Anthropology.* Trans. Claire Jacobson and Brooke Schoepf. New York: Basic Books.

Makarius, Laura
    1969   "Le Mythe du Trickster.'" *Revue de l'histoire des Religions* 175: 17-46.

Pelton, Robert
    1980   *The Trickster in West Africa: A Study of Mythic Irony and Sacred Delight.* Berkeley: University of California.

Propp, V.
    1968   *Morphology of the Folktale.* Trans. Laurence Scott. Austin: University of Texas.

Radin, Paul
    1972   *The Trickster: A Study in American Indian Mythology.* New York: Schocken Books.

Radway, Janice A.
    1984   *Reading the Romance: Women, Patriarchy, and Popular Literature.* Chapel Hill: University of North Carolina.

Stallybrass, Peter and Allon White
    1986   *The Politics and Poetics of Transgression.* Ithaca: Cornell.

Stewart, Susan
    1978   *Nonsense: Aspects of Intertextuality in Folklore and Literature.* Baltimore: Johns Hopkins University Press.

Toelken, Barre
    1976   "The 'Pretty Languages' of Yellowman: Genre, Mode and Texture in Navaho Coyote Narratives." Pp. 145-70 in *Folklore Genres*. Ed. Dan Ben-Amos. Austin: University of Texas.

Turner, Victor
    1969   *The Ritual Process: Structure and Anti-Structure*. Ithaca: Cornell.

Wiget, Andrew
    n.d.   "His Life in His Tail: The Native American Trickster and the Literature of Possibility." (unpubl. ms.)

Wolkstein, Diane and Samuel Noah Kramer
    1983   *Inanna: Queen of Heaven and Earth*. New York: Harper and Row.

DECEPTION AND WOMEN
A RESPONSE

Edwin M. Good
Stanford University

0.1   In responding to the articles in this volume one by one, I wish first to attend carefully to the way the author has worked out her thesis, the scholarly argument to the end. Secondary is the question of the adequacy of the thesis in each case. Where I have questions about that, I find that almost always I wish the thesis were a bit more radical than it is—a conclusion that is to me both fascinating and surprising. Doubtless some of my colleagues, both male and female, will find it surprising as well.*

1. Three Radical Women: Tamar, Yael, Ruth

1.1   Johanna W. H. Bos sets out to show how, as "counter-type-scenes," the stories in Gen 38, Judg 4:17-22, and Ruth 3 portray their feminine protagonists as both autonomous individuals and as subverting patriarchal value-assumptions. Without question, we must accept her demonstration of the autonomy of Tamar, Yael, and Ruth.

1.2   Tamar's move from passive waiting in her father's home, through the realization that, though Shelah has come of age, she has not been offered his husbandly services, to her ruse of dressing—and acting—as a prostitute in order to force Judah to deal with her, and her shrewd insistence on precisely the gifts she demands, together with the beautifully dramatic suspense of the dénouement and Judah's recognition, wonderfully portrays autonomous action. The narrator, of course, passes over the act's risks. Conveniently, her fertile period that month coincides with Judah's trip to Timnah, a serendipity that fiction is allowed but fact might have lost. Conveniently, in the intimate embrace of whore and customer, the customer fails to recognize his partner (another instance of his "not seeing," even though he is, as Bos remarks,

---

* I wish to express my gratitude to Cheryl Exum for her gracious response to my excited wish to contribute to this volume of *Semeia*.

at the פתח עינים, the "entrance to Enaim," as even the JPS version prosaically renders it—or the "opening of the eyes" [par. 2.4.4]). Perhaps she concealed her face with a veil, though our narrator says nothing of it. Perhaps it is rather a sideways comment on how easily, in such patriarchal groups, superior men might think inferior women beneath their notice. Father-in-law has married Tamar to two of his sons and told her, no doubt with a kindly pat on the head, to wait with her Daddy until the next son is big enough, but he has never *seen* her clearly enough to recognize her even in intercourse.

1.2.1 One could hardly be more decisive than Yael, and if autonomy consists of acting in decisive distance from authority, implicit or explicit, she is autonomous. Ruth, too, fits Bos' thesis, for, though she obeys Naomi's proposals in ch. 3, she does so in her own way. Naomi could give her an outline of actions, but the talk in which the actions must issue could not be prearranged, and there Ruth handles herself with exemplary intelligence and humane sensitivity (and Boaz responds to the latter, 3:10). There is surely more than a smidgeon of luck in the story, and again the narrator passes over it. How was it, in ch. 2, that Ruth happened to land in Boaz' field? How did anyone know that another woman would not be at Boaz' side at the threshing-floor festival? We don't ask. Still, Ruth's initiative has enabled the proper conclusion to come about.

1.3 But it strikes me as a nice question whether the ingredient of deception in the stories—one of the structural members of Bos' account of the "counter-type-scene" (par. 1.4)—will allow the conclusion. That Tamar, Yael, and Ruth are successful in their endeavors, and that those successes undercut some precious patriarchal suppositions, seems an unexceptionable conclusion. That the means by which the successes come about is best labeled deception seems to me doubtful. Tamar, to be sure, deceives Judah, and he deceives himself, even to the point of sending his sidekick to look for the wrong kind of prostitute. In a sense Yael deceives Sisera in not telling him that she does not necessarily buy her husband's political alliances. Yet is not her deception as much a matter of not informing Sisera that his lordly warrior's habit of ordering women and other subordinates around will backfire on him this time as of letting him think she will do only what he tells her to do? I wish Bos would say just what counts for her as deception or deceptive action. I am not quite persuaded that Yael is the deceiver; like Judah, Sisera deceives himself with his easy assumptions of male prerogatives. Yael uses that self-deception for her own ends, in the autonomous way that Bos portrays. As for Ruth, I simply cannot see deception at work in ch. 3 at all. "Keep it private," is the effect of Naomi's advice and of

Ruth's and Boaz' agreement. But private is not the same as ruse. That Ruth arrives after Boaz has fallen asleep is happenstance. It is not at all clear that she intended to do so.

1.3.1 I do not think that this disagreement with Bos undercuts her suggestion (par. 0.4) that the successes come from the women's use of strategies available to them, the strategies of the less powerful that nevertheless accompany the somewhat surprising autonomies. But perhaps the overstatement in her category of deception is an overstatement of the powerlessness.

1.4 Though recognizing that an element in the available strategies may be sexual, Bos seems to underplay it. Of course, she does not do so in the case of Tamar, where the sexual embrace is the center and pivot of the entire transaction. But with Yael, we have only hints of it in the reading, such as the remarks about "opening" and "covering" in pars. 3.2.2 and 3.2.3. Yet is not that "pressing" (par. 3.4.3) invitation to Sisera, "Turn, sir, turn to me, don't be afraid" (4:18), more pressing than mere politics would dictate? And does not the combination of that warmly repeated invitation to "turn to me" with the verbs of opening and closing suggest an implicit sexual promise? Perhaps that is where the deception enters. The sexual aspect has been somewhat submerged in Judg 4, to be sure, but the poetic version in Judg 5 is more nearly explicit, describing Sisera as "slumping, falling, lying" בין רגליה, "between her feet" (5:27). But I would reject Lagrange's emendation of 4:21 quoted in par. 3.2.5, which has Sisera falling "between her knees" (בין ברכיה). Bos specifically prescinds from an overtly sexual interpretation of Ruth (note 7 and par. 4.3.3.7). But I am not satisfied with the alternatives she mentions. That the narrator is "serious" rather than "suggestive" (note 7 following Campbell) seems to me a *non sequitur.* And that the references to sexuality in Ruth 3 have to do with "business" rather than with "romance" (par. 4.3.3.7) seems a false dichotomy. To be sure, marriage in those days involved contractual obligations, and the transaction between Ruth and Boaz deals with them. But the contract and Boaz' promise to pursue it are not incompatible with the implication that the night spent on the threshing floor was not passed merely sleeping, and the harvest context as well as the way Ruth's coming to Boaz at that place is narrated make entirely normal the assumption of sexual relations. Nor, I would argue, is it "irrelevant" to the story at all, for here Ruth, like the other two women, acts out her sexual being in the course and in the interests of her decisive action in this problematic situation.

1.5   So I am not satisfied that Bos has made her case for deception as the strategy by which the women overcome their contextual weakness in winning through to their successful conclusions. Nor do I believe that she has taken sufficient account of the ways in which their autonomy is sexually expressed. As I read those episodes, the sexually explicit and implicit actions or attitudes suggest that, paradoxically, it is precisely in their acting with and against men *as women*, as sexual beings in their own right, that Tamar, Yael, and Ruth accomplish their decisive autonomies.

2. Tricksters

2.1   Naomi Steinberg brings us back to deceit through the figure of the trickster. It is fascinating to follow her through the trickster literature, and she is surely right to suggest that this mercurial concept badly wants a great deal of refinement. I wish I did not have to say that I think her own account of biblical tricksters is a bit narrowly conceived and itself wants the subtlety of refinement. Perhaps she was trying to show just one or two types of tricksters, but she does not say so.

2.2   She does well to remind us that "trickster" is as much a scholarly construct as an indigenous phenomenon. I for one had forgotten that. Nor is the construct merely modern. The Tricky Slave is a staple of classical New Comedy (e.g. Menander and Plautus), and from there came by direct routes of readers and, perhaps, players to Shakespeare. Whether comic actors in classical times specialized in stock roles, as they evidently did in Shakespeare's time, we cannot know. Were certain actors regularly cast in roles like that of the Tricky Slave? An answer might tell us much about the public perception of such indubitably "trickster" figures.

2.2.1   What troubles me about Steinberg's very brief discussion of biblical tricksters is that she flattens out the character to mere deceit, with the comment, "Whatever attention biblical scholars have paid to the trickster in the literature of ancient Israel has typically focused on the use of deception by women" (par. 2.1). There are many reasons to criticize biblical scholars, and, if Steinberg is right, this is one of them. But it is not encouraging that Steinberg herself focuses there, with a nod to male deception on the side.

2.3   I am not persuaded that deceit is simply identifiable with trickery. If it were, any lie would qualify its teller as a "trickster." But Abraham is not being a trickster in Gen 20 when he tells Abimelech the lie that Sarah is his sister. He is being merely a liar, trying to keep his wretched skin intact. That God must step in to correct Abimelech's misapprehension and set the matter straight seems to me sufficient indication that we do not have here a trick that turns a situation of power upside-down. Abimelech acts soberly and straightforwardly in restoring Sarah to her husband and in giving her "brother" (the one bit of humor in the episode) a little something for his trouble (Gen 20:16). Where is the trick? Where is the outlandish and role-reversing behavior? I can see it much more readily in the rather more skeletal version of the story in Gen 12, where Abraham first pulls the stunt on the Pharaoh—or unfairly orders Sarah to pull it and put herself in jeopardy. There at least the chauvinistic audience might well have laughed that Abraham got away with bilking the Pharaoh of some wealth. The effect of the gift of silver to Abraham in Gen 20:16 is quite opposite, showing Abimelech's righteous and high-minded responsibility as considerably more impressive than the patriarch's self-serving timidity. Given that outcome, the thought of Abraham's lie as a role-reversing trickster's act is inconsistent with the tone of the whole.

2.4 Do we not need a *trick* in order to have a proper trickster, a humorous reversal of power? Steinberg's illustrations of the trickster from African and North American cultures seem to suggest that those figures, theriomorphic or not (and most of them are, from Coyote on), play jokes, that part of their appeal is not only in breaking boundaries but also in the humorous ways by which boundaries, whether of social constrictions or of mental straits, are breached. But I see few humorous trickeries among the examples in par. 4.1. Perhaps the episodes of the midwives in Egypt (Ex 1:15-19) and of Rachel's menstrual syndrome qualify (Gen 31, of which Steinberg gives a nice, if brief, account in par. 4.2). I think I would identify Samson as the trickster figure rather than Delilah. But perhaps that points up the issue in thinking of the trickster as deceitful. There seems no deceit in the episode of Judg 16:1-3, for instance, and yet the humorously unexpected feat of strength by which Samson leaves the Philistines lying in ambush with—as we must imagine—their eyes bugging out was a trick worth playing!

2.5 Steinberg's suggestion about the instability and vulnerability of those in power (par. 5.22) is a very interesting one. But what about a story like the Tower of Babel? Does not Yhwh act there at least somewhat like a trickster? To be sure, from our vantage point, the tower-builders in Shinar are not Yhwh's match. We are much too easily influenced by the dogma of divine omnipotence. Yhwh's own remark (Gen 11:6) suggests that they might succeed in their technological insulation from the divine. But the solution is, as I have argued elsewhere, humorously understated: don't knock them sprawling all over the landscape but quietly remove their means of cooperation. It does not necessarily portray a weaker power overcoming a stronger. But confusion of the language is the kind of thing a trickster would do, and if the story circulated among Judahite exiles in Babylon as a bit of underground humor (notice the sarcasm about Babylonian building materials—lousy brick and bitumen as opposed to good, solid, Palestinian stone—v. 3), the thought of Yhwh as underdog God of underdog Judah might be implicit.

2.6   I wish I could be more positive about Steinberg's article. It strikes me as a prospectus for further research, and as such it is very provocative and interesting. She herself seems uncertain that the trickster figure will tell us a great deal more about women in the Bible than about men, and I share that uncertainty. We need much more work on this as on other comic aspects of the Bible.

3. Deceptive Goddesses

3.1   Carole Fontaine provides, I think, some of the work that Steinberg proposed as needed. I have no difficulties with Fontaine's basic thesis or the argument, and only a few qualms on details of her treatment.

3.2   First a mere question: Do we *know* that texts that narrate tales about goddesses tell us about their cultures' understanding of women? By the same token, can we be sure that what a culture says about gods informs us about what it thinks about men? I have not seen the evidence—or have I just missed presentation of it?—that this transfer from divine female (and male) to human female (and male) corresponds to certain knowledge. I am willing to entertain the idea, but it seems that I am invited to do more than entertain it. It is almost as if I look around and discover that I have, by whom I know not, been betrothed to it.

3.3   I enjoyed Fontaine's discussion of the Inanna-Enki contest over the *me*, a text that I have chuckled over for many years. One of the problems I have with Proppian analysis, however, is that it is sometimes difficult to distinguish among questions of genre ("divine journey," in this case, par. 3.11), *topos* (e.g., the relation of Inanna to Enki, par. 3.2), "type-scene" (e.g., banquet-contest, par. 3.4), and "character reading" (e.g., Donor, Villain, Innocent Persecuted Heroine, etc., par. 3.3 for example). And where in all of that does the identification of a trickster have bearing? Or does the trickster float freely among them all? Are we helped more by thinking of a "divine journey" genre than by thinking of a "banquet-contest" type-scene? I incline to think not. If we are concerned with Inanna as trickster, does it really matter that she changes "character reading" from (self-)Dispatcher to Donor to pursued Hero? It matters, I think, that various male roles are occupied in this text by the female Inanna (if there is an answer to my question above, par. 3.2). But does Fontaine propose that trickster figures typically shift roles as their tales move along? I never find her suggesting that someone is a Trickster, for example, *rather than* a Donor. Ought Propp be redacted so as to include Trickster as a "character reading"? These are, I emphasize, questions.

3.3.1 I wonder whether that wonderful tale about Inanna's squirreling the *me* off to Uruk from Enki might not be a kind of character-parody. One thinks of Enki as trickster sometimes (e.g. his sidelong message to Utanapishtim in the flood story of the Gilgamesh Epic), but here Enki is on the receiving end of trickster-ish activity. If Inanna occupies male roles, is this one of them, a matter of hilariously out-Enki-ing Enki?

3.3.2 Indeed, I wonder whether this text might represent a quite special type-scene. Fontaine points to the "banquet-contest," and to several examples of Enki in particular as the loser in them (par. 3.4). Perhaps one of the conventional *topoi* of the banquet-contest is that Enki is the butt of the contest. So the question is not whether his "guard is down," as Jacobsen defensively suggests, but that females sometimes turn him, as Fontaine remarks, almost in passing, into "the foolish Lord of Wisdom" (par. 3.5).

3.3.3 But is it really a case of deception? I don't see that it is. It is a case, to be sure, of "diminished capacity" on Enki's part, if I may borrow that term, in which Inanna's capacity is distinctly not diminished. But she does not sneak the *me* away from Enki; he gives them to her, one by one, in formal presentation. That he is susceptible to drink may be part of the humor of the banquet contest. But the point is surely that she shows herself more intelligent in the situation, more in command of herself, more competent, than "wise" Enki. She doesn't trick him; if anyone tricks anyone, Enki tricks himself. Inanna bests him squarely, and, using her powers later to defend her boat against the attacks from his change of heart, she bests him again to the point where he acknowledges and participates in her victory. Is that not the humor of the trickster's trick, that our laughter arises not from the underhandedness of the victory but from its straightforwardness? To be sure, the culture seems to say, the female's victory is a surprising, and therefore funny, reversal, as males are supposed to win. I wish I could point—perhaps Fontaine can—to a text in which a male bests another male in such a banquet contest. A somewhat horrendous instance from another culture entirely is the Thyestean feast that lies behind Aeschylus' *Oresteia*. The Samson instance that Fontaine adduces (Judg 14:10-20, par. 3.6) is different from the Inanna-Enki text in two ways: first, a female *does* deceive Samson into losing; but second, the hero loses, in effect, to the other males. But it is not quite the instance I would like, because of the intervention of Samson's bride. Indeed, we need some instances of banquet contest with no female participants in order to argue the point that Fontaine wants to make, that the female must make use of powers of weakness in order, surprisingly, to overcome the male. *All* of the instances we see are of feminine success, and it almost begins to look as if an element of the type-scene or genre is precisely feminine victory. That might make the victory less humorous, the status of the female less precarious. The beautiful parallel to the Inanna text that Fontaine draws in Judith 12-13 (par. 3.61) is surely not in the slightest humorous.

3.4   I am less well acquainted with the Hittite Inaraš myth, and I have questions only about one of the terms of the analysis and some of the parallels to Hebrew materials. The former is the use of the Proppian "Donor Test" terminology (pars. 4.4–4.41). The episode referred to, where the goddess gives sexual favor in return for assistance, seems to me rather distant from any point where she is Donor, and the Proppian analysis appears to add rather than subtract complication. Of course, there are desirable complexities, but a Token Male may be allowed a wistful reference to Ockham's razor. Moreover, down in par. 4.5 Fontaine seems to change her mind about the "Donor Test" in the Hittite case.

3.4.1   As to biblical parallels, I am not persuaded that in Gen 38 Tamar is *required* to give her favors to Judah (par. 4.4). On the contrary, as Bos convincingly showed, Tamar is acting autonomously and at her own volition in the prostitute ruse. She is the one who wishes to become pregnant. Indeed, here is one of only two texts I can think of in Hebrew narrative about which Fontaine is mistaken in saying that texts "condemn women and goddesses when they attempt to initiate sexual exchange" (par. 4.4). They certainly do, but precisely not in Gen 38 and not, in my reading, in Ruth 3. In fact, is not one differentiation between Gen 38 and 39 a thematic opposition that structures their juxtaposition, the rejected wife who morally plays the prostitute in Gen 38 and the wife who immorally plays the rejected prostitute in Gen 39? Moreover, ought we not to think of passages such as Song of Songs 2:17; 4:16; 7:10-13; 8:14 as counter-instances to the claim later in the same paragraph of moral condemnation of females who say "Come! Lie with me"? I would point to the Tamar-Judah story again as the contrary evidence to the statement that "Villainy" characterizes female seduction of men, where men's demand for sex as payment for assistance is but a normal test (par. 4.41). That story, to be sure, is contrary to a great many conventions in the Hebrew Bible and elsewhere, which is why it is so inexhaustibly fascinating. Again, the comparison of the fate of the dragons in the Inaraš myth to Sisera and Yael in Judg 5 (par. 4.6) seems to me a bit stretched, in the sense that the dragons are done in by the Helper in the Hittite story, but Yael does not function as Helper (pseudo-Helper, perhaps, or anti-Helper) in either Judg 4 or 5. A better comparison, it would seem, is the Esther-Haman feast, which equally well points out the ambivalent character of the hospitable female, though both Sisera and Haman would have to be characterized as Despicable Men.

3.5 I am back to the question of deception, then. Do we need to be somewhat more precise in identifying what counts as deception? If additional precision helps us to gain a clearer perspective on how these cultures perceived the female, it will serve the cause.

4. Wise, Strange Tricksters
4.1 It is a long while since I have been made to work as hard by a reading of anything as by Claudia V. Camp's powerful, subtle musings on the conjoined and opposite females in Prov 1-9. Among other things, the essay sent me scurrying to a note pad to scribble the outlines of a completely new perspective for me on the Yhwh speeches in Job—not insignificant for a chapter yet to be written. That was contribution only to me. What this reading of Prov 1-9 does for all of us is merely to change the passage from a banal, conventional, moralistic homily to a presumably pious young male into a superbly provocative slant on the world.

4.1.1 Perhaps my only question is whether Camp really needed the trickster figure. I mean that question not biographically but literarily. As a mental exercise, laying the phenomenologies of trickster figures over female images in Prov 1-9 might be one of those imaginative experiments we all do, to the benefit of our scholarship, from time to time. Sometimes such an experiment results in our seeing with the alien structure what we could not see without it (I think of my own experience comparing the structure of Aristophanic comedy to the stories in Daniel in "Apocalyptic as Comedy: The Book of Daniel" in *Semeia* 32 [1984], 41-70). Whether or not the juxtaposition is justifiable historically or philologically, it works and we use it. Sometimes the alien structure shows us something that is there even without the demonstrative intervention of that structure, something that works even if we lay aside the occasion in which we first saw it. From what she herself says (par. 6.10), Camp has used the trickster idea in this way. Thinking about it showed her some things about Prov 1-9 that she had missed before, things that allow a quite new sense of what the passage might mean, but they are there whether or not one expounds the trickster myths. She could have shown how they work without the trickster material, though it does no harm that she used that material.

4.1.2 Why am I not sure that Camp needed the tricksters for this reading? It is partly that she keeps reminding us that the fit is not exact, that especially the hilarity of most trickster myths is absent from Prov 1-9. I have raised that point before in this response, and the fact that there are traditional trickster tales without the usual comic atmosphere (Camp points to only one, par. 0.22, and I cannot from my own knowledge add any) does not really damage the point. If the Bible has adopted tricksters into its ambit, it has transformed them, it seems, eliminating a sizable amount of what makes them in other cultures *trick*sters.

4.2 I continue to have some small difficulties in detail with some of the applications to Biblical matter. When, for instance, Camp claims (par. 1.3) that Judith, like Tamar and Ruth, "break[s] [her] society's boundaries on sexual behavior in order to accomplish good for [herself], for society, and, ultimately, for Yhwh," I have the problem that I cannot see that Judith breaks any sexual bounds. When she is left alone with Holofernes, he is dead drunk and quite incapable of sexual activity, and she promptly kills him and spirits away his head. She allows Holofernes the impression that she is willing to break sexual bounds, but she is not actually brought to the test.

4.2.1 The discussion of Gen 3 (pars. 4.3–4.32) most intriguingly pushes that passage past the obvious ways the tradition has read it. To move it away from the dogma of Original Sin is all to the good, and to question Mendenhall's idea of the critique of wisdom is a positive step as well. But it seems to me that Camp has dropped back into a unitary reading of the passage. And her descriptive rather than condemnatory reading bañalizes it. Perhaps Gen 3:14-19 "describes what every Israelite knows to be the nature of existence" (par. 4.31), but it does a great deal more than that. Must we not see this passage too as multi-dimensioned and with multiple meanings? Surely the disobedience to a specific command is contained therein, but at the same time, Yhwh is responsible for the intolerable situation that leads to it, and he overstates the penalty. The snake overstates the positive prediction of the outcome, but is not really mistaken about it: their eyes are opened (3:7) and they are said to have become "like [God], knowing good and evil" (v. 22). Whether or not the snake is wrong in saying that the deity is afraid of the humans' acquisition of knowledge, clearly the deity wishes to prevent their getting it, or else the prohibition is only a test (which is no more acceptable here than in Job). Wisdom is attractive to the woman, and it does come to be part of the human condition, but at a cost. Because the humans have wisdom, they must leave the Garden. Yes, human wisdom is condemned as a trespass on divine territory, but it is also described as part of the human condition. The divine command is justified by reference to divine authority, but it is also called into question by its incoherence with human ability to think (and notice that only the woman thinks in this passage [3:6]—Adam certainly does not). The description of the human (and reptilian) existence in vv. 14-19 is, of course, not an unrealistic one, but it is not merely a rehearsal of "what every Israelite knows," even though every Israelite does know it. It is also, and most obviously, a series of curses. Gen 3 seems to me, then, an exceedingly complex, multi-layered myth that cannot satisfactorily be read in any unitary way but that requires a multiple reading. Indeed, I think it requires a deconstructive reading, as the conjunction of opposites is one of the clearest characteristics of the text. Being no Hegelian, I find no over-arching *Aufhebung*.

4.3 These objections are minor and picky. Perhaps the one on Gen 3 is not just picky. When an entire article presents such subtle and widely multiple readings, one is surprised to find the multiplicity apparently falling away in one place. Otherwise, the way in which the multiplicities in Prov 1-9 are drawn and teased out is most illuminating. To turn the Strange Woman (an odd term, and I wish Camp would speculate more about it) and Woman Wisdom into a single but not unitary or univocal figure is a neat piece of maneuvering, which wonderfully lights up a text that, except for a couple of vivid patches, had become old and tired to me. The nicest thing about Camp's achievement here is the way in which the conjunction of the two figures and the conceptualizations and images that go with them spell the deconstruction and evaporation of moralism which is so dead a weight otherwise in Prov 1-9. And all without rewriting the text or pretending that there is in it what is not there!

4.4 Finally a word about the feminist concluding reflections (pars 6.1-6.22). Camp's political justification of a hermeneutics of suspicion (par. 6.2) strikes me as being not merely adequate but thoroughly apt. There is no place that is unreachable by the patriarchal power structures, and even the anti-structures of the liminal margins can be turned to their advantage. Camp recognizes the risk in either abandoning the center to the traditional power or taking up the political cudgels in order to live in the center of the culture, and I think she states the risk precisely. What fascinates me about her proposal about the feminist embrace of the hazard is its comic view of the world, a view that laughs in both negation and affirmation, both denial and reconstruction, that accepts critique and admiration. "From woman is the beginning of sin." Of course that is a misprision of Gen 3, and far from the only one. "As in Adam all die" (1 Cor 15:22) is another. Can the tricksters, the comic brigades of our age, male and female alike, accept and reject both in the hilarity of a world most ridiculous when it takes itself most seriously? "She" is a completely adequate generic pronoun. I'm not yet willing, however, to abandon "him" entirely. I would rather pull a "Camp" trick, refuse to choose between them, and use them interchangeably. It might be a start on the language of the new age.

5. Politics and Language

5.1 Esther Fuchs is not fooling around. Her essay is tough and tough-minded, relentless in its logic, and compelling in its carefully considered stance. I had a curious kind of S-curve reaction as I read. The thesis, that language reflects a patriarchal political ideology, strikes me as unexceptionable and undeniable. As I went further into Fuchs' reading of Gen 31, I became uneasy with what seemed a careful but skewed attention to the story, so that the text appeared not necessarily to demonstrate the thesis. But then I came to see that it does demonstrate it—but not univocally or, strictly speaking, necessarily—and that the problematic to which Fuchs points is a quite devastating one to biblical theology. I see no point in wasting time repeating Fuchs' thesis about language and male power, with which I find no difficulty. I want to raise some problems about Gen 31 and its environs, first contentiously in relation to her thesis and then in a more comfortable connection with it (how comfortable Fuchs will find it, I don't know). Finally, I will suggest what I see as a catastrophic theological issue, catastrophic not because I particularly dislike it but because it seems to me devastating to the religious traditions in which it is an issue.

5.2 Every reading of every text, I presume, is skewed. None of us ever has the last word with a text, unless the text is so shallow that its possibilities can be exhausted. That is not the case with Gen 31. That I find Fuchs sometimes missing points that I think I see is no triumphal whacking off of her head. She sees points that I have missed too, and I would rather not have my head whacked off. We can talk, I mean to say, and I would like to do so.

5.2.1 That Gen 31 is a crucial episode in the Jacob story (Fuchs, par. 1.2) is certainly so. It proposes a kind of closure to the series of deceptions by Laban, though an ambiguity remains to which I will return below. That that closure, however, represents any sort of cap to the deception between Jacob and Esau seems to me quite impossible. For when we come to the reunion of those two in chs. 32-33, we see that that reunion, detailed and motivated as it is, with Jacob's feisty message (32:5-6), his terror at Esau's approach, his careful deployment of a procession of gifts and family members to keep Esau occupied before he gets to Jacob, his obsequious behavior (33:3), is not exactly straightforward. Esau attempts to turn down the gifts, and Jacob likens seeing him again to "seeing the face of God" (vv. 8-10), a sight that in the preceding episode gave Jacob both a limp and a blessing. The phrase itself, then, as we the readers know, is extremely ambiguous and, indeed, misleading, deceptive in Fuchs' definition. Moreover, Esau proposes that they go back to Seir together, and he will slow down his pace so that Jacob's flocks and children can keep up. Jacob deceives Esau again with the assurance that he will go there and his refusal of Esau's proffered convoy (vv. 12-15). And as soon as Esau is out of sight, Jacob slips away to Succoth and thence across the Jordan to Canaan and Shechem, "safe," as the text has it (vv. 16-18). That is to say, Jacob is still deceiving Esau with false promises and misleading expectations. Ch. 31, then, is in no sense at all a closure to the earlier Jacob-Esau episodes, and the manner of Jacob's dealing with Esau sets a serious question against Fuchs' contention that the point of this chapter is "to dramatize Jacob's moral transition from a cunning Ya'akov to an upright Israel" (par. 4.4). If in chs. 32-33 Jacob is still cunning, then he has made no moral transition. Though he becomes Israel, he is not "upright" Israel but, throughout chs. 32-33, "uptight" Israel.

5.2.2 That points for me to the aspect of Fuchs' reading that I found most surprising: she takes everything Jacob says and does quite at face value. It almost seems as if her case with Gen 31 depends on supposing that either Jacob is portrayed ambiguously and ironically or Rachel is, but both cannot be. For example, I find Jacob's speech to Leah and Rachel, vv. 5-13, ironically pious in the extreme. He claims a revelation from God in a dream as justification for his breeding practices, narrated in 30:37-43. But ch. 30 made no reference to divine inspiration, and why should we believe one here? Jacob is clearly both angry at and afraid of Laban in his somewhat careful statement (31:5) that Laban's "face" is not as it was before, and the anger is justified by the statement of cheating (v. 7). But Jacob thinks he has done no cheating of any sort, and his success in breeding is now ascribed not to his shrewd manipulation of the breeding environment, as 30:37-43 had it, but to divine intervention. Why should we accept this astonishing piety here? Especially if, as one could argue, Leah and Rachel did not. Fuchs argues that Jacob's reference to divine intervention puts him in a better light than the women's somewhat crass economic reasoning in

vv. 14-16 (pars. 2.1-2.3). I suggest that we can read it in the opposite way: that his references to God are a smokescreen, and that his wives bring him down to earth by exposing his real motives. In that case, the dialogue, far from "exonerating" Jacob of the suspicion of economic motives (par. 3.1), underscores them, and so does his excessive generosity in his gifts to Esau in ch. 33. To be sure, Leah and Rachel agree with Jacob's evaluation of their father's attitude. But Jacob is not thinking so single-mindedly of Laban's good as he claims. His eye is distinctly upon his own advantage, and his return to Canaan, in response to the divine command, needs acquiescence from the women. Jacob himself deceives them in his manner of presenting the case for departing, and with no more credible explicit motivation than Rachel's motivation for taking and hiding the household gods. The argument that Gen 31 presents Jacob in a moral transition seems to me exceptionally weak, and I think Fuchs depends on it much more than she ought. It seems to motivate her saying that Jacob is "incensed" at Laban's accusation of theft of his gods (par. 4.2). The text does not say so, though it is careful to say in v. 36 that he is "incensed" (JPS) at the entire situation, with Laban rummaging around in his, Jacob's, tents with nothing resembling a search warrant. I do not think we can reason in a straight line from "curse" to "incensed," in a culture where curses were much more objective than we think of them, and, more significantly, I am not persuaded that we can read v. 32 as rhetorically a "curse."

5.2.3 Just as I do not find persuasive the contention that Jacob undergoes moral transformation in this (or any) chapter, I think Fuchs misses a tone of truculent distrust at the end of the passage. What she calls (par. 5.1) "conciliatory speeches" by Laban (vv. 43-44, 48-53) seem to me just the opposite. The "covenant" into which these two groundpawing bulls enter is not conciliation but is the establishment of watchful hostility. Laban first lays claim to the women, the children, and the flocks, then throws up his hands in resignation and proposes a monument of "witness," something that will stand there objectively and to which appeal in strife can be made (vv. 43-44). Then he invokes the divine name as one who "watches" (צפה) between the two, one who spies on Jacob's treatment of his wives (v. 50) and who keeps the two hostile camps separated from each other (v. 52). I should argue that this truculent covenant leaves the deceptive relationship between Jacob and Laban just where it has been all along, closed only in the sense that the deception and the mistrust are out in the clear where everyone can see them, but not in the sense that they are removed.

5.2.4 But let us not have a "Witness Pillar" between Fuchs and me about Gen 31. In responding to some other papers, I have expressed my delight at the increasing possibilities of multiple readings. If my reading of Gen 31 deconstructs Fuchs', then hers deconstructs mine. If I cannot see that Jacob comes out of Gen 31 smelling quite so sweet as she seems to think, I cannot also argue that our narrator has cast Rachel in a more positive light than she thinks. Indeed, I suspect that in the end Gen 31 deconstructs itself, forbids any unitary reading that tries to get anyone, Jacob, Laban, Rachel, or any of the others, to look at all good. That raises some questions about her contention that this chapter demonstrates the patriarchal power to exalt the male and denigrate the female. But if the chapter does not exalt the male, it certainly does not exalt the female either. The question is whether denigration by means of an excess of motivation, as with Jacob and Laban, is preferable to denigration by a paucity of motivation, as with Rachel and Leah. Maybe no denigration is preferable. But there we are in a world quite different from the one the Hebrew Bible gives us. In fact, I think Fuchs takes us afield from the point in some of her contentions. Take, for example, only the argument that the *niddah* laws of Lev 15, especially as they refer to menstruation, tie into this systematic denigration of women. Perhaps they do, but in order to make the point stick, it is necessary to deal with the fact that the law detailing the "uncleanness" of menstrual blood (Lev 15:19-24) is preceded by two laws that detail the "uncleanness" of semen, both in sexual intercourse (v. 18) and in any other ejaculation of semen (vv. 16-17). If the purity laws show that menstrual blood causes "horror" in men, they show that semen does too. I do not wish to claim that men are denigrated in the Hebrew Bible as much as women are, for I do not think so. But the grounds on which any claim about it are to be made must be carefully examined.

5.3 And that brings me to my last point. Fuchs does not need me to say that she is dead right in the claim that "An awareness of the interdependence of heterosexual politics and biblical narrative is the first step in a feminist critique of the patriarchal claim to absolute 'objective' truth" (par. 7.3). She is right in thinking that this awareness must inform both literary critics and "biblical feminologists." Exactly who the latter are is not entirely clear to me, but that probably does not matter. As she goes on to speak of the risk of validating androcentric epistemology, it seems to me that she points to a different problem from the one that is present with literary critics. The literary reading of biblical material entails a basic fairness to the texts themselves, to readers and their worlds, and to the stimulation of conjunctions and disjunctions between readers and texts. I do not think that literary criticism has to do with the sort of "truth" or, perhaps better, "truth claim," to which an appeal to epistemology points. When Fuchs refers to discourse in the "biblical academy," I read her as moving in some sense into the theological and religious realms of discourse.

5.3.1   And there is the problem. Androcentric epistemology and androcentric discourse, taken together, are a theological problem. The more I read the Bible (whether in its one-volume Jewish or two-volume Christian version), the more I am persuaded that it is (or they are) irredeemably androcentric. There may be a few pockets of variance, such as the inclusion of male domination as part of the curse in Gen 3:16, but they are the more notable for their rarity. What Fuchs proposes, then, seems to me to imply the theological program either of replacing the Bible as the ground of Jewish or Christian religious authority by something else or of recasting it in some thorough-going way to reflect the basic feminist claim to truth.

5.3.2   If she is right that (1) the Bible is androcentric and (2) androcentrism is an unacceptable construction of the world—and I believe she is right on both counts—then the Bible has ceased to be either an adequate ground of authority for religious truth or an adequate source of religious insight. If it has lost validity in either sense, because it is at best partial in its construction of the world, then Biblical authority is dead, and feminism has killed it. Feminism has done what Deism could not do, what liberalism could not do, what many modern efforts to modify Christianity's sense of the basis of its truth failed to do.

5.3.3   Am I just being dramatic? (By the way, I am absolutely not being sarcastic.) No, I do not believe so. From the first glimmerings by which I began to see the justice in various forms of the feminist critique of the traditions of our world-view, I thought it would probably come to this. As the consciousness has risen, and I have gone on reading the Hebrew Bible in the course of professional duty, I have become more and more certain of the hopelessness of the task facing anyone who wishes to give a positive feminist reading of the Bible. I think there is no way that it could be welcomed intact into the feminist orbit. I would rather occupy a generous, morally acceptable feminist construction of the world than stick by a religious authority that is characterized now as it always has been by a disagreeable bias and an illegitimate occupation of power.

TRICKY THEMATICS

Mieke Bal
University of Rochester

1. *The trick of thematics*

Composing a volume of essays on the basis of a theme is a gesture based on a number of assumptions. One assumption is contained in the idea of theme itself: a theme is a semantic unit, and the recurrence of such a theme can be measured only if one knows with certainty what the theme is. Since a semantic unit is not a given but a construct, the criteria for defining a theme are dependent on the interpreter who, in turn, will rely on other, often unconscious assumptions which are taken to be "natural" certainties. The idea of female wit or trickster is such a semantic construct. In this response, I want to show some of the problems inherent in the thematic enterprise which the authors of the papers in the present issue could not avoid. They can hardly be blamed for it since, as I will argue, the endeavor itself of a thematic collection holds slightly contradictory aspects. The major problem is the positivist illusion implied in thematics. Under the spell of such an illusion it becomes extremely hard, even for feminists, to avoid, let alone to undermine, some of the sexist biases that are part of our culture and its scholarly endeavors.

The positivist illusion and sexism easily go hand in hand, as the following example shows. During a conference on thematics, held in Paris in 1985,[1] Claude Bremond offered the example of the *cocu* as a case for a translistorical thematics. All over the world and all through literary history, he argued, the theme of *cocuage* recurs in literature. *Cocuage*, however, is defined as the ridicule of the victim of female adultery exclusively. Defining a theme in those terms, which betray the assumption of sexual possession of a wife and the idea of ridicule attached to the wife's autonomous erotic behavior, is one way of excluding the counterpart of this theme: the equally recurring theme of

---

[1] A selection of the papers of this conference appeared in *Poétique* (1986). My own critique of the positivist claim of thematics was rejected for publication. Claude Bremond gave as his argument for that decision the opinion that themes have no gender. Obviously, such had not been my claim at all.

male adultery and the consequences, not so much ridicule but serious nonetheless, for the "betrayed" wife. Now it is not inherently *wrong* to define a theme as *cocuage;* it is true that there are many stories in which we can recognize the theme. But the very gesture of defining it does preclude a clear view of other cases of sexual "unfaithfulness" in relation to this variant. In other words: accepting unproblematically the definition of the theme, the thematician is no more innocent of the ideological assumptions contained in it than are the writers who use the thematic tradition to inscribe their own version of the theme. Both confirm the theme's assumptions and ignore its symmetrical counterpart which becomes obscure, deviant, and is virtually forgotten.

Unlike the theme of *cocuage*, the theme of the trickster is neither burdened with moral judgment nor a priori gender-bound. Yet, similar ideological biases are inevitably attached to it, as I hope to show in this paper. Both themes are represented by characters, unlike, for example, themes like "death," "time," or "afterlife," which can be represented in various forms, of which character is only one possibility. As soon as themes are character-bound, they become subject to the same ideological influence as characters in general. Characters almost inevitably have a sex,[2] and therefore, they are necessarily subject to the ideologies of gender. A first attempt to classify possible trickster-figures shows this problem. For example, it seems rather obvious what sort of a character a trickster is: a morally and sometimes ontologically ambivalent being who plays tricks that deceive others, often for the good of the community. If we try to categorize characters on the basis of such a definition however, it turns out that agreement is not easy to find. Thus few readers of the Bible will object to the idea that the woman in Gen 3 behaves like a trickster when she tricks the man into eating the forbidden fruit.[3] They might or might not agree to assign the same status to the serpent. But few would agree that the deity, in the same story, acts also like a trickster. Yet the definition fits better the serpent and the deity than the woman. The bad reputation the woman has received in later readings bears witness to her problematic status as a trickster: little is left of her ambivalence. God, when s/he[4] defines the conse-

---

[2] I insist on "almost," since sometimes sexless characters are assigned a sex in subsequent readings, while their sexlessness seems relevant. The serpent in Gen 3, for example, is ostensibly sexless. It cannot be denied character-status, since it speaks and acts in the fabula. In medieval paintings, it is often represented as female. This identification of trickster and victim is one of the strategies of the sexist use of the story.

[3] In *Lethal Love* I argue that it is wrong to call the beings who act at this point in the story by the names they receive later. Naming is part of the strategy of reading that fixes the unfixed, thus pushing the sexism inscribed in the story.

[4] The use of the androgynous pronoun s/he is neither a feminist joke nor a rigid application of the use of inclusive language. As I have argued in *Lethal Love*, the deity's androgyny

quence of eating from the forbidden tree in terms of the human condition, on the other hand, is more deceptive than the woman, when she simply gives the fruit to the man after finding out that it was good. The similarity between the behavior of the serpent and of the deity, who both define the consequence of the transgression in terms of human life, though the one more positively, the other negatively, points to the similarity in status of the two characters. Hence, both are tricksters or neither is. If the deity is not classified as a trickster in the same way other characters are, this reticence is due to the respect for the "real" god[5] that is projected onto the character. Similarly, the eagerness to assign to the woman the status of trickster is due to the contempt of "real" women,[6] believed to be deceptive by nature, rather than to the actual behavior of the character in Gen 3, onto which that contempt is projected. The idea of a thematic unit "trickster" promotes the reader's belief that there is an objective category of characters that contains the one rather than the other of these three characters. Hence, thematics potentially supports sexism in that it obscures the reader's awareness of his or her own interpretive decisions.

This critique of thematics does not imply that I find the endeavor of this issue of *Semeia* pointless. It is crucial to bear in mind the relativity and interpretation-boundness of themes while discussing them. If we do so, it becomes possible to examine the theme as a dynamic, readerly unit that can exemplify reading in general, especially the reading of ideological texts like the biblical stories.[7] The enterprise of "reading tricksters" then, becomes an example of how reading affects, and is affected by, previously acquired assumptions. Such an analysis would lead the critic to ask questions about assumptions underlying the essays in this volume. For example, although most authors briefly

---

is an important issue in the development of the similarity between divine and human beings which is one of the major points of the story. At the moment when God utters the prohibition in Gen 2:17, the human being is not yet sexually differentiated, and can thus be called androgynous. God's likeness to the humans, stated not only in 1:27 but again in 3:22, therefore implies "hes" or "hir" androgyny.

[5] I mean by "the real god" the image of God people believe in, as opposed to the deity as a character in a story written by authors whose belief was not necessarily identical to that of modern believers.

[6] Here, too, I mean by "real women" the image of women people believe in, not the properties of women as they really are. The image of women held by the authors of the biblical stories is, again, not necessarily identical to the one modern men believe in (and which does or does not coincide with beliefs on women held by modern women). Esther Fuchs rightly stresses the importance of this distinction.

[7] I use the expression "ideological texts" or, rather, "ideo-stories" in a specific way. I mean by it those stories that feature easily structured pairs of binarily opposed characters, a simple event that can easily be evaluated morally, and a mimetic form that is easy to visualize. As a result of these features, ideo-stories lend themselves better than other, more complex stories, to ideological manipulation. See Bal, 1988b.

raise the question of gender, it is taken for granted that tricksters are often female characters. Esther Fuchs' paper is the only one in which the author systematically compares female and male tricksters in order to grasp the ideological function of the genderedness of the theme. The assumption that tricksters are often female is based on, first, a definition of trickery, second, a selection of cases, and third, an interpretation of those cases. For example, Johanna Bos analyzes three stories of female deception. Her definition of tricksters remains implicit but can be derived from the beginning of her essay. The three characters she discusses are "successful in what she sets out to achieve" and belong to "a weak group" (pars. 0.1 and 0.4). Later, the author suggests a connection between the subordinate position of women and their deceptiveness. Defined in this way, deceptive characters must be subordinate characters. Yet in the story of Yael's murder of Sisera, it is not at all clear that the trickster is of a lower status than her victim. Thus, there is a gap between definition and selection. This is even more striking if we take the case of Ruth into consideration. It seems extremely doubtful to me that Ruth deceives Boaz. She can hardly be described as morally ambivalent—insofar as she actually *is* described as such, those descriptions are the result of readings from a male bias, and should not be taken for granted.

The analysis in fact indicates that the only remaining feature of the type is success. The attempt to draw attention to successful, smart, and indispensable female characters in the biblical narratives, which in general display a male ideology, is part of a feminist endeavor: to pull women and their roles "out of the shadow." But showing that women do have a place in culture is not enough. A genuinely critical analysis of their specific roles requires not only a feminist thematics but also a critical methodology. Although some of the authors show a keen awareness of this problem (Camp, and to some extent Steinberg), such a methodology has been unevenly developed in the essays of this issue.

2. *The tricky trickster*

The concept of trickster and the concept of language as defined by modern semiotic theory have much in common. Both are inherently ambivalent, and both are tricky. In his seminal book *A Theory of Semiotics*, Umberto Eco defines a sign as anything that can be used in order to lie. The production of a semiotic unit called "trickster" can be seen as a literary representation of such a view of the sign. Tricksters are, as most of the essays agree, morally, religiously, philosophically ambivalent creatures. This *ambivalence* characterizes their being. *Deception* is what characterizes their behavior, hence, their narrative function. This function is, then, to exemplify semiosis in its central characteristic. Seen in this light, tricksters function as a *mise en abyme* or metasemiotic figure (Dällenbach; Bal, 1986). In the promotion of the welfare of the community lies their *social usefulness*. As Claudia Camp argues, tricksters are indispensable to enable a culture to interpret and overcome its own dichotomies, contradictions, and suppressions. And in their very trickiness lies their semiotic meaning: they are a sign of the sign. They represent the essence of language, the very language their existence depends on for their representation. This paradoxical status of the trickster may be its most fascinating and culturally valuable aspect. An analysis of particular trickster-stories needs to take this feature into account.

The most interesting remarks in the essays are those where this relation between trickery and semiosis or language is thematized. Here lies the best of Fuchs' essay, for example, and in general the recurrence of this topic in most of the essays gives a welcome sense of unity to the volume as a whole. The most successful of the essays in this volume is not only the one that does so but also the one whose topic superposes one more layer of language/trickery onto the double one of linguistically represented tricksters: Camp's analysis, not of a trickster character, but of the *imagery* of tricksters. As a first exercise in the enhancement of ambiguity that I would like to promote as a methodological a priori (see also Culler, 1983), I will use a sentence from the beginning of her essay to show the semantic exuberance that results from such a superposition.

To begin a comparative essay on tricksters with the warning that one should not "[succumb] to the siren of comparison" (par. 0.1) is not only a first-class nicety, but also good pedagogy. There is no better way to *show*, rather than to *tell*, what trickery is about.[8] The phrase is a figure of style, a paradox, as well as a narratological trick, a *mise en abyme* or mirror-story; it is a logical problem of the order of the phrase, derived from Paul's first letter to Titus, vv. 12 and 13: "all the inhabitants of Crete are liars," said the Cretan prophet.[9] It is a strategy of seduction, reassuring the readers who might be worried by the very endeavor of the paper, yet carrying it out; it is, in fact, a trick, and as such it is a characteristic example of the properties of both tricksters and language. Let me explain what I mean.

---

[8] The opposition between "showing" and "telling" is an allusion to the dichotomy, commonplace in literary criticism, which was initiated by Plato in his distinction between *mimesis* (showing) and *diegesis* (telling). See Genette for a fine analysis.

[9] The prophet, by the way, is a trickster-character whose conspicuous absence from the usual lists of tricksters is evidence of the problem of thematics discussed in section 1. The structural similarity between Yael's ambiguous response to Sisera's indictment (Judg 4:20) and the ambiguity in Deborah's prophecy in 4:9 shows that the two types are indeed characterized by the same use of language.

First, the reunion of various semiotic units under the thematic heading of "deceptive character" or "trickster" is a comparative act. Comparison is the basis of thematic behavior: it is on the basis of a comparison between units that one decides to categorize different units with the same label. Warning us against the seductions of comparison, Camp enters into a logical dilemma she can only escape by undermining the category she is shaping, hence, the comparative basis of her analysis. As a paradox, the figure draws attention, promoting the alertness of the reader.

Since the essay itself is comparative nevertheless, the warning contains a mirror of its broader context. In narrative theory, such a mirror-story is called a *mise en abyme*. The functions of such a figure are prediction, allegorization, and displacing the interpretation. This is exactly what the figure is doing in relation to Camp's essay: the author will, indeed, pursue her comparative endeavor without, however, *simply* succumbing to its risks of easy and tricky thematics. Hence, the figure predicts the conclusions. It allegorizes the latter, too: in inserting a female image of a trickster, the siren, in the figure, the author assigns to comparison a status as slippery, as tricky, as the subject of the essay, the *imagery* of the trickster which is, of course, something quite different from the character of the trickster itself. And the figure displaces the interpretation of the essay from "trickster imagery" to "tricky imagery," to the (ideological) trickiness of the idea of imagery. The comparison we read in the figure at first sight is a methodological gesture; but slowly, imagery itself becomes synonymical of comparison: an image *is* a comparison.

Any approach to a concept as tricky as that of (linguistic) tricksters that intends to do it full justice needs to cherish the ambiguities it implies. Tolerance toward ambivalence and ambiguity, difference and instability, is a precious asset of the critical analyst. At the same time, and in order to compensate for this seemingly anarchistic attitude, methodological awareness is needed. And in order to decide which methods will be the most fruitful and reliable for tricksterology, a view of the trickster that goes beyond thematics is crucial. Under these conditions, and only then, can one avoid the fallacies inherent in naive thematics, counter its positivistic bias, and neutralize its tendencies toward sexism, anachronism, and paronto-centrism.[10] In the following section, I will briefly review the essays in order to assess the extent to which they show this indispensable openness.

---

[10] The term "paronto-centrism" has been suggested by Margaret Alexiou to express a fallacy parallel to anachronism, ethnocentrism, and androcentrism: the tendency to take the present as the norm, and assess the implications of events and behavior in the past in terms of evolutionism.

3. Considerations of method

The papers by Johanna Bos and Esther Fuchs, opposed as they are in their conclusions, have more in common than appears at first sight. Both analyze Hebrew stories of female tricksters, remaining within a literary method and drawing strong conclusions related to contemporary feminist issues. The other three essays differ from these two in that they are more interdisciplinary, drawing upon anthropology, and intercultural, using to some extent the comparative method or at least a concept of culture against which to view the stories. Although they discuss feminist methodology, their conclusions are less directly focused on non-academic feminist issues. On the other hand, their awareness of the methodology of women's studies is keener.

As I have already suggested, I see in Johanna Bos' essay a typical instance of the consequences of the non-reflective use of a thematic label. Her paper, which consists, in fact, of three rather autonomous essays, remains therefore within the boundaries of a traditional view of deceptive characters. It is based on the assumption that texts are more than reflections of a social reality (par. 0.3); they are thought of as social agents, actively influencing actual social developments. This assumption is less common in other disciplines than theology. In literary studies, for example, such a relationship between text and society has long been shunned as a genuine taboo.[11] It is the merit of feminist criticism to have made a convincing case for the acceptance and, indeed, crucial importance of the analysis of such a relationship. That analysis is not only vital for a meaningful understanding of specific, i.e. religious, texts, but also for our insight into the functioning of language and, more in general, of signs.

The manner in which Bos elaborates the relationship between text and society is complicated by another distinction she makes: that between the text in relation to social reality on the one hand, and the text as a religious message related to a specific section of social reality, i.e. the religion of a community, on the other. Thus she distinguishes the effect of the female deceivers' activities in promoting patriarchal society—an obviously problematic consequence of the first relationship—and their effect in promoting the "divine promise"—a positive consequence of the second relationship. She posits an opposition between those two effects, a negative and a positive one, support for patriarchy and for Israel, as if the separation were self-evident. This religious bias spoils

---

[11] After a long tradition of biographical and historical criticism, the movement of New Criticism posited the autonomy of the literary text. This movement was clearly related to political liberalism. Sociological approaches to literature have never really succeeded in overcoming the resistance introduced by New Criticism. See Culler (1983) for an account of this debate, and, for example, Jameson for a successful political approach.

the effect of the strong claim made from the feminist perspective about the social meaning of texts. The same problem also appears in Phyllis Trible's work (1978; 1984). The effort to "redeem" the texts, which are initially criticized for the sexism they express and promote, inevitably leads to contradictions and obedience to traditional views. In contrast, Esther Fuchs' work (e.g. 1985a and 1985b) shows that an uncompromising critical attitude cannot but ultimately reject the texts (this conclusion will be nuanced later in my commentary).

A second problem of Bos' essay is the methodological eclecticism. The three parts of her essay—I like to think of the "three essays," inasmuch as they are so distinct and so little interrelated—follow a different method. This certainly helps against the monotony of mechanistic application of one method. But it impedes the comparability of the results. In the case at hand, this is a serious flaw; how can we know to what extent the subject of the three parts is homogeneous under these conditions? Moreover, the literary approach chosen is presented as "different emphases," said to have arisen from "the differences among the narratives themselves." This justification of the methodological variation rests on the assumption of New Criticism that texts are autonomous wholes which "speak for themselves" (par. 1.1). That assumption implies autonomy, not only from social reality, but also from the reader. When carried through to its extreme consequence, this claim is untenable, especially from a feminist perspective. It entails invulnerability of the texts and might promote the positivistic fallacy that posits the truth of the interpretation. Thus, it also protects the "truth" of sexist interpretations which are based on the same claim, or method, or assumption.

A third problem is the relation between text-type and method. Since all three texts analyzed are narratives, the results would gain in consistency if the methods chosen related to the genre. This is the case for the second story only.[12] The first story is divided into five units (par. 2.3.1). Neither the criterion for this division nor the choice for the number of units is argued. The division seems to function only for the subsequent line-by-line exegesis. The quality of this exegesis is uneven; some remarks are very suggestive, e.g. the idea that Judah's vain search for Tamar is expressed in refrain-like repetition, and the importance of the anonymity of the report on Tamar's whereabouts, reflecting, I would add, the essential anonymity of the prostitute she is accused to be. But the traditional method prevents systematic insights. For example, had the author used in this case the same method as in the second section, she would have been able to assess the importance of *focalization* in the representation of Judah's misjudgments in relation to

---

[12] Bos' source for narratological analysis is my Dutch text; I take the liberty here to refer to the more extensive English version (Bal, 1985).

Tamar's right judgment. The similarities in structure between the Tamar story and the Yael story—both play on ambiguity, Tamar of her own status as a woman/*qedeshah*/*zonah* and Yael of Sisera's status as a man/no man (Judg 4:20)—would have enriched our understanding of *female* trickery.

A quite revealing instance of the problem of method and its consequence for the feminist value of the analysis is in the statement that Judah's condemnation of Tamar is "unusually harsh" but that he had the right to decree her sentence (par. 2.5.11). The remark evokes the problem of the social reality the text is said to reflect and to transcend. I would suggest it does nothing of the sort; it *responds* to a social reality. Indeed, the story of Tamar can simply not be understood without at least minimal knowledge of social reality. How else can we make sense of the implications of levirate marriage, as central in this story as it is in the book of Ruth? But then, the fact that Judah had the right to decree a sentence on a rejected daughter-in-law, and for the crime of "harlotry" which he was free to commit himself, cannot be simply stated; the existence of that right is part of the conflict between the social and the religious message. I must say that I have trouble seeing how this conflict can be solved, and it seems necessary at least to acknowledge and criticize it. The powerlessness of the critic who cannot go beyond the simple statement shows that the method—literary criticism—if applied to ideological texts, leads to a form of criticism that we call *paraphrasis*: a criticism that remains within the ideology of the text that is therefore basically uncritical. These remarks are not meant to suggest that the paper is useless. I can see this type of analysis function within communities of women who try to draw support for their lives from the biblical narratives as models for their own behavior. My criticism only affects the status of the analysis as an academic feminist endeavor.

If I find that Bos' feminism suffers from a religious bias and the resulting idealistic view of the texts, as well as from insufficient attention to the relations between social reality and literary form, Esther Fuchs' essay shows the possibilities and the limits of the opposite attitude. I find it more successful, yet basically flawed. Fuchs' uncompromising critique of biblical ideology and her relentless anger toward the (academic) culture that uncritically accepts and repeats it are refreshingly liberating. That such an attitude entails other biases is unavoidable and acceptable as such. My problem with the essay is one of method: of literary analysis and of feminism.

The literary method is not falsifiable. The analysis of the story of Rachel's theft of the *teraphim* and the far-reaching generalizations the critic draws from it are based on a negative description of the text. The "suppression of explicit indices of motivation, the suspension of authorial judgment, and the absence of closure" are the features of the text which Fuchs takes as her starting point (par. 1.1). Where do these three negative features come from? The standard for this clearly normative view of the text is double: internal, in the comparison with male trickster figures; and external, in modern literary theory, in its turn derived from modern conceptions of what a literary text should be. The first of these two standards is acceptable, but it is not systematically applied. If Rachel's theft is not motivated explicitly, Yael's act is less enigmatic for example, and commentators show little doubt about Delilah's motivations. The general condemnation of Delilah and the common ambivalent attitude toward Yael must therefore rest on other norms which it is important for a women's studies perspective to clarify. The genderedness[13] of the lack of motivation is therefore not sufficiently argued. The other possible explanation, the self-evidence of the *righteousness* of Rachel's act, is not considered. I will argue later how this self-evidence, and the resulting positive interpretation of Rachel as a worthy wife of Jacob and participant in Israel's endeavor, can be assumed without contradiction. Motivation is a tricky criterion: it is motivation itself that needs motivation (see Culler, 1975). In other words: if an act or event is motivated, that situation means that it was in need of motivation, hence, not self-evident. In this sense, Jacob's tricks require perhaps more motivation because their embedding in the divine plan was a new issue superimposed on an old folk-story. The interpretation of the lack of closure is equally unjustified; Rachel's act is simply part of the more comprehensive event of the departure from Laban's estate, which was not yet finished.

The second standard, derived from modern literary theory, is anachronistic and can in principle easily lead to bad criticism, including sexist interpretations. The theory in question, gap-theory, was introduced in biblical scholarship by Meir Sternberg and Menakhem Perry in a famous article of 1966, published again in Sternberg's book (1985). I have tried to argue elsewhere (1987) that the method allows ideological biases to intervene unnoticed. In Sternberg and Perry's article, this is the case, for example, when the authors wonder whether Uriah, in 2 Sam 11, *knew* that his wife had been "unfaithful" to him. It can hardly be said that the victim of David's sexual imperialism has willingly "betrayed" her husband in the first place. But the idea that the whole text is structured around this "basic" question comes from the assumption that sexual property was the issue, that the question of Uriah's knowledge mattered at all. There is no need to assume this. Nor do we need to assume that in the biblical narratives, the opposition

---

[13] Although the term "genderedness" may sound slightly awkward, I insist on using it. It expresses more than just a relation to gender. Genderedness means that the bias *coincides* almost with gender; that it is extremely hard if not impossible to disentangle the two.

between good and evil is invariably at stake. This moralistic fallacy, as I like to call it, underlies the most sexist interpretations of Gen 2-3. I contend, with Claudia Camp, that at least in the Genesis story this is not at all the primary issue. But then, I do not agree either that the story of Rachel's theft can be interpreted from the perspective of this modern moralism. And if I am right in this contention, then Fuchs' interpretation is anachronistic.

This lack of control over the risks of the interpretation is inherent in gap-theory; the exclusively negative definition of gaps and their resulting hypothetical status impedes any attempt to prove or falsify their presence or relevance (see Hamon; van Alphen). Apart from the question whether or not ancient texts can unproblematically be interpreted with the help of modern theories—I happen to think they can, but under strict conditions—the choice of this particular theory is a most unfelicitous one.

Again, this is not to say that the paper is therefore pointless; I can imagine that this interpretation is, as is Fuchs' stimulating and sharply critical other work, indispensable as a weapon against the abuse of *contemporary* images of biblical women. The quote from Adrienne Rich shows that this is an urgent need. Insofar as Rachel's story has indeed been interpreted negatively, Fuchs' counter-move is fruitful. As an account of the ancient Hebrew culture and its ideological biases, however, it does not stand. Why is this so serious? In spite of Fuchs' warning against the repetitive nature of much biblical scholarship, her own analysis is not beyond that risk. In remaining within the moralistic isotopy of good and evil, she repeats the gesture that has been so fundamental for modern patriarchal society: to impose on all of culture the dichotomy between good and bad as parallel to self and other, same and different. We need a solid deconstruction (Culler, 1983) of this dichotomy, if we want to overcome it, rather than a reversal of its values. The importance of a critical analysis of the "other," i.e. biblical cultural artifacts, lies precisely in the awareness of otherness that is the most powerful weapon in the struggle against both androcentrism and ethnocentrism.

Fontaine's essay on deceptive goddesses in ancient Near Eastern myth is more profoundly critical. In the first place, Fontaine does not limit her method to literary analysis, but, in contrast, uses literary analysis as a first step toward understanding the social and anthropological motivations of the stories. The basic question of the essay is precisely one which relates method, literary type, and gender: why is it that various cultures produce similar stories, in which the role of women is invariably the morally ambivalent one? The method used to argue for the similarities among the various stories, drawn from folklore analysis and structural anthropology, has the flaw that Alter's concept of the *type-scene* possesses. It is based on the analogical argument. It is a well-known problem of this structure of argument that the similarities depend on the interpreter's focus of attention—exactly like thematics. Propp's and Lévi-Strauss' models have been sufficiently criticized for it, and there is no need here to enter into that discussion (see Culler, 1975; Coward). But there are at least two strategies to minimalize the risk of the method. Firstly, the method works better when combined with other, preferably alien methods. Fontaine's implicit feminist methodology, which pushes her to go beyond simple structuring in order to *explain* the relations between a type-scene or structure and a social preoccupation like the power of women, helps overcome the limits of structural analysis. Secondly, the more refined the model, the less risky the analogical argument becomes. This was obviously beyond the scope of Fontaine's paper, and I think the material would be enriched, but the thesis not undermined, by a more thorough analysis of each of the stories.

Fontaine does not start from the premise that female characters are negative; she allows the stories to display the importance accorded to women in their symbolic behavior. Unlike Bos, she is not apologetic, taking pains to show that some women *are* important. In contrast, she takes the power of women for granted in those cases where it is clearly right to do so, showing nevertheless how the same mythical material is domesticated later when patriarchal ideology fastens its grip on the culture. That this attitude toward symbolic meaning is fruitful appears at several instances; for example, the explanation of Zipporah's action as induction of symbolic menstruation in the male hero (par. 2.0), or when the critic is able to relate seemingly diverse stories, if not to the same theme, at least to similar motifs that various themes share. This kind of suggestion is the more convincing when it concerns, as it does here, noticeably problematic passages.

As the above remark suggests already, another advantage of Fontaine's approach is her openness to historical change in the literary material. This openness helps to break through the narrow limits of strictly literary analysis, and to connect literary material to the social reality to which it responds. Refusing the too easy qualification of Inanna as a fertility goddess—a label whose frequent use is due, I think, to modern attempts to reduce the role of women even where the material shows that they actually were important—and insisting, instead, on the essence of variety in the goddess' character, she also notices the more restrictive features of later occurrences, where Inanna becomes the woman who acts successfully in a male world. The tension between one and many, in the image of this goddess, seems a typical instance of the tension between polytheism and monotheism that we see throughout the history of religions. Where monotheism reigns, the number of important secondary figures—saints, heroes, patriarchs—increases, as does the number of forms the single deity can take on.

Although I have few problems with Fontaine's approach as such— I would say that she makes the best of it, given the scope of the volume—it ends up reaching the same limits as any thematic enterprise would encounter. I will try to show what I mean with one example. Where Fontaine shows how the type of the False Bride encourages men in patriarchal society to realize that the nurturing and sexually serviceable female can also bring death, she reaches the limits of thematic/structural method. In a sense, a different kind of analysis could start here, one that would enhance differences after the analysis of similarities. Different questions then come up.

In the first place, we may wonder why it is that the mothering features and the sexual ones are so invariably related. Sisera's murder by Yael, one of Fontaine's examples also mentioned in other essays, is perhaps the most disturbing case. Mothering is there such a capital aspect that the story makes a good case. Mothering is the aspect of the encounter that "does the trick," reassuring the victim but also, as has not been noticed as often, the one that performs the indispensable function of showing the victim's immaturity, his need to undergo the rite of passage which is the model of the subsequent scene.[14] This seems so at least in the prose version of Judg 4.

The scene in the tent, whose entrance is the subject of a very revealing exchange, matches the description of Turner's concept of liminality (criticized by Bynum): confined within the narrow space of a female domain, the fallen hero arrives at the final stage of his successive abdication of power which began with his defeat, his descent from his chariot, his flight into the wilderness and his arrival at the site of initiation—represented by the no-man's land between the two armies where loyalties have become unclear. Yael's motherly behavior must be understood within this ritual event. Sisera's anxious but over-authoritative order to Yael, to answer "none" to any inquiry about a *man*'s being in the tent, can also be read as his denial of manhood, his acceptance of his childish abandonment to the powerful mother. Yael's "trick" in fact consists solely of the literal acting out of this predicament of the victim himself. The trick is more like a riddle,[15] the question then being: how can a man be no man? and the answer: a dead man.

---

[14] In my book *Murder and Difference*, I have analyzed the murder of Sisera in detail. I argue there that it is only in the "male" version of Judg 4 that the rite of passage is a relevant isotopy; in the "female" version of Judg 5, initiation is as irrelevant as the male victim as such is. The pleasure of female power outdistances the position of the victim.

[15] I analyze this exchange as a riddle-and-answer game, comparable to the riddle at Samson's wedding, in *Death and Dissymmetry: the Politics of Coherence in Judges*.

The sexual isotopy, of course, is obvious, especially when Yael puts Sisera to bed, but also when she acts within the type-scene of the wooing of the bride by offering drink, yet it is even more obviously embedded within the motif of mothering.[16] This is hardly a coincidence; the combination, mixture, confusion, or conflation, of sex and mothering in the male perspective might be the most crucial knot in the various but related causes and motivations of patriarchy.

The scene becomes even more interesting when we compare it to its lyric counterpart in Judg 5. There is no trace there of the initiation, the liminality, and the mothering. Yet the motif of motherhood is not absent. It receives a most astonishing expression in the frightening image of the fetus falling between the feet of the aborting mother. The thematic statement that mothering is a common motif in the two versions would lead to the obliteration of this sharp contrast. In fact, the lyric evocation of the bad mother, who is, however, not the deceitful, tricky mother of the epic version, is part of two networks. The one is the interrelation between sex, motherhood, and murder which motivates this triple evocation of female power. The man is only a pretext here, the object of the female exercise of power; as a subject, he is irrelevant. In ch. 4 by contrast, the woman is used by the poet to express male fright, not female pleasure. The second is that the aborting mother in ch. 5 is related to the two other mother-images in Deborah's song: the good mother, Deborah herself, whose helper Yael is, and the bad mother who is willing to give away for rape the daughters of Israel, in the final stanza.

•My point in this all-too-brief allusion to the thematic lines which cross in the Sisera-murder is not to outwit Fontaine's own excellent remarks. I want to suggest that, firstly, even the differences between Judg 4 and 5, between two versions of the *same* event, might be more important than the similarities, let alone between stories where the thematic similarities are necessarily slighter. Secondly, I want to argue that thematic analysis can also be played out against itself. Relating the image of mothering to two other images of female power, and to two other images of motherhood, is an attempt to show that in spite of problems inherent to thematic analysis, it can also be expanded, rather than abandoned; expanded in the sense of an opening on *any* level of semantization. The motifs can be considered as both contributing to the expression of the theme and producing a tension between the theme under consideration and other, competing or analogous themes. Needless to say, this kind of dynamic, open thematics allows the deeper

---

[16] Zakovitch's naivety is stunning, when he uses the *milk* Yael feeds her baby as an argument in favor of a purely (male) sexual reading of the scene. Zakovitch's blindness to the mothering aspect is in my view a compelling argument for the case I wish to make for a differentiating, problematizing reading of this and similar scenes.

questions about the causes and motivations of patriarchy in its various forms to come to the fore.

Naomi Steinberg shows in her essay that the traditions around the figure of the trickster go far beyond the Middle Eastern cultures. The thesis of her paper is that the analysis of such figures must nevertheless be situated within the particular culture in which they function. This polemic against cross-cultural analysis is useful inasmuch as similarities are usually too easily assumed. It is a warning, in fact, against the sort of thematic statements that we saw in Bremond's contribution to the thematics conference in Paris. In the essay as a whole, however, the same fallacy tends to recur. In spite of her keen awareness that gender is a relevant aspect of the trickster traditions, the fact that in the quoted African material tricksters tend to be male figures, while in her examples from the Hebrew tradition, most tricksters are female, is not explained. In relation to this problem, I find it difficult to maintain at all that most tricksters in the Hebrew Bible *are* female, or that a significant number of the female characters are tricksters. If we look only at the book of Judges, we cannot overlook the fact that Yael and Delilah have their male counterparts in Ehud and Jephthah, and their actantial counterparts—victims as opposed to tricksters—in Jephthah's daughter, Samson's bride, and the absolute victim of the entire Bible, the woman in ch. 19. Rachel's trick with her father's house-gods is more than matched by Jacob's numerous tricks. If we can consider Ruth a trickster at all, then Boaz' strategy to eliminate his rival (4:2-6) is no less cunning than her seduction.

There may be, in general though not systematically, indeed a relation between trickery and lack of power. But the opposition between the powerful and the powerless plays equally strongly between the old men and the younger generation (Jacob/Isaac) and between the high-placed and the subordinated (David/Uriah), for example. I do not mean to suggest that there is something wrong with the attention to female characters in the essays; on the contrary, I find it a bit risky to attribute the feature of trickery, with its moral ambivalence, to female characters only. It is precisely to the extent that we realize which categories of figures share with female characters the position of powerlessness *and* cunning that we may come to understand the deeper roots of oppression in general, of the need for hierarchies at all, and of the specific forms they take. Why should it be that a culture represents as powerless both its women and its younger men? It seems clear to me that the tendency of female characters to side with their younger son (Rebekah) is based on the awareness of the similarity in their situation. Siding with young men, however unreliable the position may be, is a way of specifying, of narrowing down the causes of oppression.

In the beginning of her essay, Steinberg suggests that the comical and the narrative are aspects of trickster traditions. Unfortunately, these two ideas are hardly elaborated. They both need more work to support the claim. In a way I contend that drama is the more congenial genre, and that the narrative passages in which tricksters operate have strong dramatic features. The example quoted above of the exchange between Yael and Sisera is dramatic; it is to the extent that both characters are confronted with each other that the "misunderstanding" is possible at all. On the other hand, I am not convinced that these scenes are comical. It might be the case that male tricksters lead to more comical stories than female ones, and this possible difference brings us back to the problem of definition inherent in thematics.

Claudia Camp's essay has been touched upon earlier. Her methodology is the most throughly feminist in its subtlety and its empathic yet critical perspective. Her view of the material as testimony to the culture's struggle with its own contradictions allows for an analysis from an inside perspective. Paradoxically, her awareness that we are always necessarily falsifying when studying other cultures makes it possible to adhere to a more open attitude and acceptance of the irreducible difference of the other culture than we are used to encountering in writings whose authors are so sure they understand their object unproblematically. I could quote many instances of the academic gain of such an attitude, but the essay speaks for itself.

If I were to criticise this essay, it is in its lack of literary method this time. It is useful to point out where and how literary methods, powerless as they are when they are used in isolation from historical and anthropological tools, could bring more understanding. I have suggested earlier that trickster figures are exemplary semiotic units, and as such hold a metasemiotic commentary. In turn, their status as characters broadens the scope of semiosis itself beyond the boundaries of language. The tendency to identify semiosis with language alone is challenged by other ploys the tricksters use, other "signs used in order to lie" (Eco). To analyze the subtle differences in the semiotic behavior of the figures can contribute to a more refined understanding of semiosis, hence of the functioning of culture and the lines of power within it.

Let me give an example from Camp's essay. When she cursorily mentions "that the ploys of Tamar and Judith are accompanied by deceitful speech" (par. 3.6), Camp repeats the (false) view of Tamar that male-biased commentaries have continued to spread. Tamar does not lie, at least not with speech. The liar and fellow-trickster in the story is Judah, if we consider false promises as lies (Felman). This seems a trifling detail but it is not. For the next question is: *how*, then, does Tamar trick Judah? In spite of the obviousness of her case, it is necessary to insist that her trick is a *response* to the trick played against her, not an *initiative* of trickery. There is an exchange of trickery, like a verbal exchange, a dialogue. But it is *not* a dialogue. If Tamar does not lie verbally, it is because Judah, by sending her away, denied dialogue to her.

Tamar uses the semiotic means, the signs that are left at her disposal, to take over. Her response to Judah's initiative to lie is an initiative to bring out the truth. Sexuality is one of her means, the typical one that women have left when made powerless otherwise. But her use of her sexual attraction is both exposed and hidden in a more clearly cultural, semiotic object, the veil that denotes publicly available sexuality. It is Judah who interprets her as a sign. The word *zonah* is used to indicate what Judah *thought* he *saw*. But he interprets wrongly, showing that his power over semiosis is not absolute. If Tamar were a *zonah*, his later condemnation of her would be unfair but not *wrong*, which he acknowledges it is.

Tamar continues her exploitation of culture in its most central values. Requiring, as the price for her sexuality, the tokens of Judah's sexually-based power, the signs of his patriarchal status, she gains full power, not yet of speech, but of semiosis. She possesses the signs of Judah's power. The consequence is that Judah loses, with his patriarchal power, his ability to lie. When he acts out one of the most significant instances of the double standard, condemning to death the object of his own lust, the addressee of his own sexual monologue, Tamar stops him short. She wins this exchange not by lying but by bringing out the truth, the truth that reveals Judah's lie/false promise. This is what he acknowledges, not the unfairness of his condemnation.

Tamar's provocation does not concern speech. *Discern* is the verb she uses, in the imperative, to force Judah's understanding. Indeed, her trick is about, for, understanding. It is Judah's misjudgment, his mistaken view, his failing *focalization* that Tamar acts upon, exposes, and corrects. A narratological analysis of this story, focusing on the three categories of semiotic acts involved in stories: speech, focalization, and action, brings to the fore the fundamental importance of focalization as a semiotic act, as well as a social crux. It is necessary to notice this particular aspect of the story in order to realize the possibilities and limits of male domination and female action within and against it. As a patriarch, powerful enough to replace his son's sexuality, Judah has the power to initiate deceit and to exclude Tamar from semiotic exchange. But this power is not total, and speech is not the only category of signs. As Camp so beautifully illustrates, cultures cannot afford to exclude "anomaly"—deviation from their own imposed norms, like patriarchal power—without ultimately being overwhelmed by it. Judah's mistaken focalization counterbalances his wilfully mistaken speech. This opposition between willing deceit and unwilling "deceit" is what the story displays; not verbal deceit and counter-deceit, for Tamar does not lie.

Nor does she, by the way, cause any damage to Judah, and this is yet another distinction to be made. She saves him from the loss of descendants. This evaluation of the *result* of trickery is indispensable if we want to avoid the stereotyped images so often drawn from the female trickster-figures. Tamar's act benefits Judah, restoring the patriarchal line which his mistaken protection of his son—protection and, of course, domination—had threatened to extinguish. It is the merit of Esther Fuchs' work, among others, to show that, ultimately, female success is invariably recuperated to promote the interests of patriarchy, not women's own.

Why is narratology so important in this context? It is the method which expands the domain of semiosis by enhancing other semiotic activities than speech, other signs than words. The semiotic activity of Tamar is primarily neither deceit nor speech, but didactic *demonstration*. *Showing*, as a more efficient strategy of teaching than simple *telling*, requires, within a story, focalization as its primary device. But the addressee of the teaching is the man: it is Judah who ends up *seeing right*, thanks to Tamar's work. It is Barak who, in Judg 4, closes the story by *seeing* the consequences of his earlier cowardice. Boaz must see Ruth's value, Jephthah must see his mistaken lack of confidence by seeing his daughter—if at the price of her life. Women have always been good teachers, and still are.

4. Concluding remarks

In the preceding pages, I have assessed some aspects of the five papers from a specific perspective. Although I am a narratologist, the value of the papers for me depends on the success of their feminist argument. In this concluding paragraph, I want to make more explicit why I think that the feminist value of an academic performance is *academically* speaking a fruitful standard, and how I place narratology and other methods in relation to it.

The importance of the narratological concept of focalization, and of its entire narratological framework for that matter, is due to its capacity to bridge the gap, so problematic yet difficult to avoid, among literary, formal analysis, historical and anthropological "background," and social, i.e. feminist, critique. More in general, a literary method which requires an analysis of the text as text—as written verbal unit— and as narrative—as generically specific—helps to develop awareness of the semiotic status of the object of research. This awareness helps us ask the right questions; that is, questions that can be answered at all. Since the text is practically all we have, we had better not forget its nature, its status, and its function, if we want to understand it. At the same time, the awareness of the textual status of our object and source also helps against textual absolutism; we must think about the relations between text and context on the basis of a clear view of textuality.

Let me come back to Rachel's theft, and use its enigmatic motivation or lack of it as an example of where to look, what questions to ask. Whether or not she is actually lying to Laban is not verifiable. It is also irrelevant. The text does not linger over the question, and the semiotic use of her trick is based on its very undecidability. But what Fuchs rightly asked herself is: why is this event happening, why is this particular, female, character depicted as committing this particular act? What does her role, but also its casual presentation, mean in relation to the social reality whose product and expression it is, to which it responds, and within which it functions? This question is in fact the question of what narrative means socially. Fuchs' interpretation of the choice of Rachel's trick—"I have the way of women"—as triply ambiguous is very interesting precisely because here she relates the texture of the story to the social reality—the taboo of menstrual blood—without taking it as a mere reflection of the latter. For the taboo is itself semiotic in nature, interpreting the blood as a symptom of bodily impurity, in its turn a symptom of female inferiority, in its turn a deceptive symptom of female deceptiveness. The trick itself can not be understood without this appeal to the social reality as we know it, among other sources, from the Levitical laws (Lev 15:19-33).

But neither can it be understood without the thematics of *seeing* that underlies the trick. "The way of women" is on the one hand so offensively bodily, visible; on the other hand, the "way of women" in the figurative sense (deceit? cunning? or some other characteristic?) is basically *invisible*. That is precisely why Laban is unable to see it. And why is he unable to check the truth of Rachel's claim? Because the taboo of menstrual blood is a *male* problem. A woman would simply have checked, a man would not dream of trying. Thus, the very sign of female inferiority becomes a sign of male inferiority, of male fright, a fright that blinds. This aspect entails the very ambivalence that Fuchs fails to notice and that Camp, in contrast, brings to the fore. In Camp's formulation, that ambivalence is of vital importance for a culture's survival; Fuchs' failure to take it into account therefore draws the limit of the *social*, cultural reach.

The need to account for the social background is not in contradiction to a literary analysis. I feel that the less strong essays of this volume are weaker than they need to be precisely because they unnecessarily limit themselves to literary questions without realizing that this is impossible. Rachel's act must be seen within the event in which it is embedded, the departure from Laban's estate. The departure is more than a simple quarrel, personal ambition, or need of autonomy. The entire story of Jacob's sojourn in Laban's house, from the very start, shows that the issue is a deeper, social one. Laban's claim that his daughters' children are his own is the clearest symptom of what is at stake. Laban's world is what I call a *patrilocal* world where the institution of patrilocal marriage reigns: the *beena* marriage (Morgenstern 1929, 1931) in which the daughter remains in her father's house and the husband visits her there. The power of the wife's father is near-absolute; he possesses his daughter for life, and her children are his own. The system cannot be simply called matrilinear, since the father remains the major power-figure. But the position of the son is much weaker than it is in the more usual, virilocal system.

I have argued elsewhere (1988b) that the competition between the more ancient patrilocal system and the new virilocal system is the primary source of violence in the book of Judges. The story which exemplifies this issue is also the most violent one of the whole Bible: Judg 19. It is no coincidence that it is also the most violently misogynistic story. And it is sad that it is systematically misinterpreted, even by women.[17] The act of Rachel cannot be understood without reference to its central place in the story of the transition from patrilocy to virilocy. Stealing the house-gods, an act that Fuchs has trouble interpreting, is a contribution to Jacob's cunning strategy to outwit Laban, his fellow-trickster.

If Laban tricked Jacob into patrilocy by forcing him to stay for Rachel's sake, Rachel completes Jacob's emancipation by adding to the material possessions he took over from her father's estate the symbolic tokens of the transition. The possession of the house-gods means, to this patrilocal daughter, the possession of the house, hence her right to take the child from the father and hand it over to the husband. Without this context, the act remains arbitrary; within it, it becomes comparable to Tamar's act. It is, then, a demonstration of the importance for social intercourse of a level of semiosis that the men do not *see*. Like Tamar, Rachel uses her wit for the benefit of the man, the holder of the line. This recuperation of female wit to teach the man is irritating. But it does not imply a (moral) condemnation of the woman.

Tamar was sent back to her father's house; we can now see yet another link between the two stories. Tamar was seen—wrongly—as a *zonah*. We translate the word as "prostitute," but it is not so sure that this has always been the meaning of the concept. Jephthah's mother, in the book of Judges where, in my view, the transition between patrilocy and virilocy is a constant issue, is called a *zonah* by the narrator in 11:1. But in v. 2, his half-brothers simply call her a "strange" or "other"

---

[17] In *Death and Dissymmetry*, I argue that both Phyllis Trible (1984) and Susan Niditch do not succeed in overcoming the sexist commonplaces about the story. Trible assumes too easily that the woman actually is a concubine and that the term concubine refers to a socially inferior woman, which is arguably not at all the case in the story. Niditch defends the husband's gesture of exposing his wife to rape, on the ground of three arguments, all equally falsely defensive and none of them convincing.

woman. If she were a prostitute in our sense, how could the identity of her son's father be known in the first place? If we examine all the instances of *zonah* systematically, we notice that often the sole indication of her way of life is the fact that she lives either with her family (Rahab, for example) or autonomously (the *zonah* in Judg 16:1). There are indications that *zonah* and *pilegesh*, "prostitute" and "concubine," are used interchangeably as the two terms to refer to a patrilocal woman, wife, or mother. We may wonder whether the bride of Samson, who is clearly patrilocal, would not deserve the same title, as would Delilah. If these two titles for women later received exclusively negative connotations, that is because the new system, once it has won the competition, does not like to be reminded of its less glorious beginnings. Later biblical writers probably did not even remember what the words initially meant. And still later, biblical scholars partake of this repression of the past, of otherness. In other words: Judah's mistake when he takes Tamar for a prostitute amounts to more than a simple, incidental mistake, rightly deserved by his preceding, incidental lie. It is a more fundamental lack of understanding of or a refusal to acknowledge a *different* way of life.

We can take Judah's mistake, then, as an emblem for the risks and the task of biblical scholarship. If we limit ourselves to the well-known ideas, accepting the texts only insofar as they mirror what we already know or believe, we cannot learn, and we even make serious mistakes. The systematic undervaluation of the role of women, or the underestimation of the seriousness of their negative representation against which the essays in this issue work, is a mistake that impedes the growth of insight, and hence confines the scholar who makes it to mediocrity. The acknowledgment, understanding, and acceptance of otherness, a primary feminist goal, is also a primary academic pursuit. That is why feminism is such a precious contribution to scholarship, not only for its specific insights but also for the very focus of its endeavor. I would venture that this coincidence of the feminist and the academic interests is the masterful trick of women's studies. But if feminists neglect the intimate relation between text and social reality which semiotics posits and explains, they take the risk of being trapped by their own trick, and of falling back into repetition of the age-old song of good and evil, so often sung against women.

WORKS CONSULTED

van Alphen, Ernst
    1987   *Bang voor schennis? Inleiding in de ideologiekritiek*. Utrecht: Hes Publishers.

Alter, Robert
    1981   *The Art of Biblical Narrative*. New York: Basic Books.

Bal, Mieke
    1985   *Narratology: Introduction to the Theory of Narrative*. Toronto: University of Toronto Press.
    1986   *Femmes imaginaires: L'ancien Testament au risque d'une narratologie critique*. Utrecht: Hes/Montréal: HMH/Paris: Nizet.
    1987   *Lethal Love: Literary Feminist Readings of Biblical Love-Stories*. Bloomington: Indiana University Press.
    1988a   *Murder and Difference: Gender, Genre and Scholarship on Sisera's Death*. Bloomington: Indiana University Press.
    1988b   *Death and Dissymmetry: The Politics of Coherence in Judges*. Chicago: University of Chicago Press.

Bremond, Claude
    1985   "Concept et thème." *Poétique* 64:415-23.

Bynum, Caroline Walker
    1984   "Women's Stories, Women's Symbols: A Critique of Victor Turner's Theory of Liminality." Pp. 105-125 in *Anthropology and the Study of Religion*. Ed. Robert L. Moore and Frank E. Reynolds. Chicago: Center for the Scientific Study of Religion.

Coward, Rosalind
    1984   *Patriarchal Precedents*. London: Routledge & Kegan Paul.

Culler, Jonathan
    1975   *Structuralist Poetics: Structuralism, Linguistics, and the Study of Literature*. London: Routledge & Kegan Paul/Ithaca: Cornell University Press.
    1983   *On Deconstruction: Theory and Criticism after Structuralism*. London: Routledge & Kegan Paul/Ithaca: Cornell University Press.

Dällenbach, Lucien
    1978   *Le récit speculaire: Essay sur la mise en abyme*. Paris: Ed. du Seuil.

Eco, Umberto
    1976   *A Theory of Semiotics*. Bloomington: Indiana University Press.

Felman, Shoshana
    1980   *Le scandale du corps parlant: Don Juan avec Austin ou la séduction en deux langues*. Paris: Ed. du Seuil. Eng. trans. = *Literary Speech Act*. Ithaca: Cornell University Press.

Fuchs, Esther
    1985a   "The Literary Characterization of Mothers and Sexual Politics in the Hebrew Bible." Pp. 117-136 in *Feminist Perspectives on Biblical Scholarship*. Ed. Adela Yarbro Collins. Chico, CA: Scholars Press.
    1985b   "Who is Hiding the Truth? Deceptive Women and Biblical Androcentrism." Pp. 137-144 in *Feminist Perspectives on Biblical*

Scholarship. Ed. Adela Yarbro Collins. Chico, CA: Scholars Press.

Genette, Gérard
  1980   *Narrative Discourse: An Essay in Method.* Ithaca: Cornell University Press.

Hamon, Philippe
  1884   *Texte et idéologie.* Paris: P.U.F.

Jameson, Fredric
  1981   *The Political Unconscious: Narrative as a Socially Symbolic Act.* London: Routledge & Kegan Paul.

Morgenstern, Julius
  1929   "Beena Marriage (Matriarchat) in Ancient Israel and Its Historical Implications." *ZAW* 47:91-110.
  1931   "Additional Notes on Beena Marriage (Matriarchat) in Ancient Israel." *ZAW* 49:46-58.

Niditch, Susan
  1982   "The 'Sodomite' Theme in Judges 19-20: Family, Community, and Social Disintegration." *CBQ* 44:365-378.

Sternberg, Meir
  1985   *The Poetics of Biblical Narrative: Ideological Literature and the Drama of Reading.* Bloomington: Indiana University Press.

Trible, Phyllis
  1978   *God and the Rhetoric of Sexuality.* Philadelphia: Fortress.
  1984   *Texts of Terror: Feminist Literary Readings of Biblical Narrative.* Philadelphia: Fortress.

Turner, Victor
  1969   *The Ritual Process: Structure and Anti-Structure.* Ithaca: Cornell University Press.

Zakovitch, Yair
  1981   "Sisseras Tod." *ZAW* 93:364-74.

trickster tumbles
at the edge of the world:
his face is set
toward the wilds,
but where he passes
cultures rise

women trick
inside the tent,
under the cover
of veils or night,
and on their backs
culture thrives

    Carole Fontaine

www.ingramcontent.com/pod-product-compliance
Lightning Source LLC
Chambersburg PA
CBHW031315150426
43191CB00005B/237